PRAISES FOR INSPIRED TO BE MORE

"As we go through life, we sometimes find ourselves so enthralled in the day to day challenges, we often forget to step back and just breathe! Author Colette Hope provides us with the biblical inspiration we need as we seek to fully live the life God has called us to live. She reminds us that we are God's masterpiece, designed for His purpose and His glory. If you are in a place in your life and you are ready to live the full promise of God that is waiting for you, I encourage you to read Inspired To Be More."

~ LINDA TAYLOR,
PRESIDENT AND FOUNDER OF KOACH KONSULTING AND
AUTHOR OF THE TRUTH IN YOUR HEART

"This book is filled with inspiring nuggets to empower and encourage you to do the work necessary to be more of what God has called you to be. Colette's authenticity illuminates on every page. You know instantly that she is devoted to helping you become your best self with her motivational messages of purpose and hope. It's a must read for all!"

~ SHELBY ALEXANDER GRIGGS,
AUTHOR & LIFE COACH FOR GALS INSPIRED COMPANY

"Colette Hope has used her breath to breathe life into her dream which is to provide us with a wonderful resource as we all continue along our journey called life. Inspired To Be More gently guides the reader inwards to reconnect with self in order to re-discover the love within. I use reconnect and rediscover, because as long as we have breath in our bodies, we have love inside. It is always there, however, we sometimes forget. This book is written in such a way to allow the reader to take her time, inhale the lessons and tools and exhale any emotional wounds that are hindering her growth, freedom, and self-love. Thank you Colette for being a beautiful example of love in action."

~ MISHA N. GRANADO, MPH, MS,
FOUNDER OF LOVE GROWS: THE
RELATIONSHIP CONSULTANTS

"In Inspired To Be More, Colette Hope beautifully illustrates a road map to get you to the greatness for which God created you."

~ ANGEL RICHARDSON,
AUTHOR OF IT'S NOT A SECRET TO SUCCESS

INSPIRED To Be More

21 Divine Inspirations for Becoming a Better You

Colette Hope

HOPESPEAK

Inspired To Be More

Published by Hopespeak Publications
P.O. Box 710338
Houston, Texas 77271-0338

All Scripture quotations, unless otherwise indicated, are taken from the *Holy Bible*, New International Version® 1973, 1978, 1984 by International Bible Society. Used by permission of Zondervan Publishing House. All rights reserved.

Scripture quotations marked NLT are taken from the *Holy Bible*, New Living Translation, copyright 1996, 2004. Used by permission of Tyndale House Publishers, Inc., Wheaton, Illinois 60189. All rights reserved.

Scripture quotations marked KJV are taken from the *Holy Bible*, King James Version, Cambridge, 1769.

Cover design by CJ McDaniel, Adazing Design

Editing by Kathryn Marion, www.ExecutiveSelfPublishing.com

Author photo by Enobong Houston, Arts Houston Photography, www.artshoustonphotography.com

ISBN 978-0-9884607-0-6

Copyright © 2012 by Colette Hope

All rights reserved. No part of this publication may be reproduced, stored in a retrieval system, or transmitted by any means–electronic, mechanical, photographic (photocopying), recording, or otherwise– without prior permission in writing from the publisher.

Printed in the United States of America

SPECIAL SALES

This book is available for special quantity discounts when purchased in bulk by corporations, organizations and church groups. For information, please e-mail info@authorcolettehope.com or visit us at www.authorcolettehope.com.

DEDICATION

This book is dedicated to my oldest and dear sister, Andrea, who is now an Angel in Heaven. After you left this earth, God revealed to me the reason for a vision He had given me even before you got sick. He spoke to my spirit and said, "I am going to use the way your sister died to teach you and women around the world how to live."

In 2004, you took your last breath on this earth, but you continue to breathe in and through me today. You are the hope and inspiration that inspires me to keep writing and speaking and spreading God's Inspired Word to the world. As you inspire me, I pray to inspire women and children throughout the earth. I will always love you and cherish every precious moment God blessed us with by having you in our lives.

~ Love, your baby sister

CONTENTS

Introduction: It's Time to Wake Up! 1

Inspiration 1: Inhale Abundance
Embracing All That Is Available to You 13

Inspiration 2: Inhale Gratitude
Cultivating an Attitude of Thankfulness 23

Inspiration 3: Inhale Grace
Accepting God's Unlimited Favor 33

Inspiration 4: Inhale Love
Embracing God's Unlimited Affection for You 43

Inspiration 5: Inhale Hope
Holding On, Patiently Expecting 53

Inspiration 6: Inhale Faith
Stepping Out On the Promises of God 61

Inspiration 7: Inhale Patience
Waiting and Trusting that God is in Control 73

Inspiration 8: Inhale Peace
Finding Serenity in the Midst of it All 83

Inspiration 9: Inhale Joy
Enjoying Your Everyday Life 93

Inspiration 10: Inhale Strength
Drawing in God's Divine Power 101

Inspiration 11: Inhale Freedom
Living Life with No Boundaries 111

Inspiration 12: Inhale Humility
Developing Your Servant's Heart 121

Inspiration 13: Inhale Balance
Centering Your Life Around What Matters Most 133

Inspiration 14: Inhale Wisdom
Becoming Wiser with God's Discerning Word 143

Inspiration 15: Inhale Confidence
Believing You Have What It Takes. 153

Inspiration 16: Inhale Authenticity
Removing the Masks to Unveil the True YOU 163

Inspiration 17: Inhale Courage
Moving Forward in the Face of Fear. 173

Inspiration 18: Inhale Perseverance
Refusing to Give Up When Life Gets Tough 183

Inspiration 19: Inhale Purpose
Discovering Your Unique Path and Walking It 193

Inspiration 20: Inhale Passion
Living Life on Fire for God 205

Inspiration 21: Inhale Greatness
Becoming More Than You Ever Imagined You Could Be 213

You Were Born To Soar! 227

About The Author: Colette Hope 231

Let's Stay Connected 233

ACKNOWLEDGEMENTS

This is my first book and it feels like I have been writing it my entire life. I have to first thank God, Who gave me the vision to write this book a decade ago. Yes, you read that right—a *decade* ago. It took me that long to stop running from what God was calling me to do, but I thank God that He never gave up on me. Thank you God, for blessing me with the privilege to encourage and empower women and kids around the world with Your inspired Word.

Next, I want to thank God for my adoring son, Donnie, who always finds a way to make me laugh. Thank you, son, for putting up with my long days and nights of being locked up in my room writing and asking you to be patient with me. Thank you for being understanding of the sacrifice we both had to make to birth this dream into reality. I could not have done it without you. I know that God has so much in store for your life and I thank Him for blessing me with the number one son in the world! I love you, Sweetie.

To my parents, Vernell and Earnest Johnson: Your love and overwhelming support is always just what I need. Thanks for instilling in me a love for Christ from the time I was a child. Thanks for always being there for me and your grandson. We appreciate your love and support.

To my big sisters, Carolyn and Daphne and Andrea (in Spirit): Thank you for the childhood memories and the life-long stories we have shared together. We have been through many things together and we are stronger and more resilient because of it.

ACKNOWLEDGEMENTS

We are not only sisters, we are true friends, and that bond will never be broken. I thank God that we are both blood sisters as well as sisters in Christ.

To my nieces (Alexis and Breanna) and my nephews (Deandre, Terae, Damian and Daylan), I love you all very much. Always remember that you were made for greatness and you can do anything you set your mind to.

To Tricia and Joy, my girlfriends and sisters: Thank you for the hours of conversation we have shared and your continuous support and inspiration. Thanks for believing in me always.

To Jackie, my girlfriend and sister: Thank you for stepping in to be my stylist and making sure I looked fabulous for my photo shoot.

To Joyce, my girlfriend and sister: Thank you for always stepping in to help me in any way that I needed.

To Dr. Dennis W. Young, my Pastor: Thank you for allowing me to lead the Children's Story Ministry at MCBC for 20 years and counting. It is in this role that I discovered my gift and passion for writing and speaking.

To all of my MCBC Family: Thanks for always encouraging and inspiring me to write a book and share my gift with the world. Thanks for being my extended family and showing my family love and support when we lost our sister, Andrea.

To My Book Project Team: Thanks a million to Kathryn Marion (my editor), Jean Boles (my proof reader), Julie Csizmadia (my interior designer) and CJ McDaniel (my book cover designer).

ACKNOWLEDGEMENTS

You all helped take this book from dream to reality and bring it to life!

To My Extended Family and all of my friends: Thanks to everyone who has ever encouraged and supported me in writing this book. You don't know how your kinds words and simply saying something like, "I'm waiting on that book," has helped to keep me on track. Thank you for your continued support and prayers.

INTRODUCTION:
It's Time to Wake Up!

It was March 2004. I had just put my three-year-old son, Donnie, to bed and was now in the midst of my nightly ritual: a hot bubble bath. The room was dimly lit with candles and filled with a sweet aroma. I normally read a book while I soaked, but there was nothing "normal" about this night. You see, we had just laid my oldest sister, Andrea, to rest. She had died at the young age of forty-one of an autoimmune disease that attacked her lungs.

The landscape of my life was now changed forever. My family and I had not been prepared for this. Andrea did not have a long battle with this disease; she had only been suffering with it for a few months. We had not known much about the disease, but from what we learned through research was that, in most cases, it could be managed and controlled. We thought my sister would surely recover and live a full life.

Andrea first became ill after a summer vacation trip in 2003. She had scraped her arm during one of the rides at the water park. About two weeks later, when it had not healed, we convinced her to see her doctor. He was puzzled with her condition and ordered extensive tests. We didn't think much of it, but very soon, more symptoms began to arise.

INTRODUCTION

More doctors' visits came along with more tests and more symptoms. Almost overnight she started having shortness of breath. *What is this? She's never had asthma before.* She was sent home with an inhaler, more medication, and appointments with more doctors for even more tests. She saw specialist after specialist, puzzled every one of them, and was misdiagnosed multiple times.

But, finally, after about six months, a name was applied to what was going on: sarcoidosis. *Sarcoid- what?* I rushed home to research this mystery disease. It is an autoimmune disease in the same family as lupus, where the body turns on itself instead of protecting itself from foreign intruders—the body begins attacking its own organs. All organs are susceptible to sarcoidosis, but primarily it affects the lungs.

The prognosis for this disease is not too bleak, I tried to convince myself. Sure, there's no cure for the disease, but in most cases it can be managed. Having a strong foundation of faith, we would have it no other way. We called out the prayer warriors, declared victory over the disease, and believed by faith that our sister would go on to live a productive life in spite of it.

A couple months later, I was at work when I received the call—the kind of call no one wants to receive concerning a loved one. One of my sisters was sobbing on the phone, telling me to get to the hospital right away. Andrea had passed out a couple of days earlier and had been in the hospital—now she had taken a turn for the worse. Within 24 hours of that call, we had lost her; she was gone forever. Her struggle was over—but ours was just beginning.

Up until this point, it really had not sunk in for me that Andrea was gone. My son had been very close to her, and now I had to hold it together for him. Once he was safely resting in bed and I was alone in my bubble bath, the tears began flowing...and, it seemed, would never end. The tub seemed to be the perfect place to cry a river of tears—the water flowing from my eyes would simply merge with the bath water.

This ritual bath was the one piece of "normal" I tried to hold on to in the midst of this tragic situation. The bottom had fallen out of my world. I was dismayed and bewildered beyond belief. Was this real or just a sick joke being played on me? Would I wake up from this nightmare to discover that this had been just a figment of my wild imagination?

I tried to pry open my eyes through the blinding tears to see if I would awaken from this bad dream. But it wasn't a dream; this was my new reality. My world would be different from here on out. Nothing would ever be the same again for me or my family.

Suddenly, a thought ran across my mind: it was my turn to do the children's story on Sunday. I had been delivering children's sermons during worship services at my church for years. The children come out from the congregation and sit on the stairs at the front of the church sanctuary where I would tell them a story about God. Andrea had often joined me to help keep the children in order while I spoke.

The thought of me being up there without her was too much to bear. No, there was no way I could do it; I wasn't strong enough yet. I would just call Pastor and let him know that he needed to cancel it or find someone else to do it.

INTRODUCTION

At that moment, God spoke to my spirit. The message was very clear and distinct, as if He were standing before me. He told me that I *would* do it, that the Holy Spirit would be with me, and that He would give me the strength to get through it. Before I could protest, God went on to tell me that not only would I deliver a message that Sunday, but that He had an even greater message for me to deliver to the world.

Months prior to my sister becoming ill, God had given me a vision to write an inspirational book which would use breathing as a metaphor for its theme. As I cried out to Him that night, God revealed to me the reason for the book and that theme. He would use the way my sister died to teach the world and me how to live.

This book is part of His divine plan.

THE MIRACLE OF BREATHING

In the last stages of my sister's life, Andrea had become very aware of her breath—she had not had a choice, because her breathing was restricted. She could not lift her arms to put on her clothes or bend down to put on her shoes without gasping for air. At that point, she had to rely on a breathing machine, and take it with her everywhere she went.

We often don't fully appreciate something until it is lacking or completely removed from our lives. How many times have you ever stopped to focus on the fascinating miracle of your breath? Go ahead and do it right now.

Close your eyes. Draw in a deep breath for four counts and hold it for two seconds. Now slowly release it for a count of eight. As you breathe, think about this miracle of life that keeps you and sustains you. Appreciate it. Thank God for it. Breath is God. Breath is life, and without it, there is no you.

There is much to be learned from this too-often-taken-for-granted process called breathing.

Using breathing as a metaphor, God's Word is to your spirit what oxygen is to your body—it is life, and without it you cannot live fully. God wants us to learn to depend upon His Word in every area of our lives. His Word should become as vital to you as the air you breathe.

The Bible was written by man but it was inspired by God. God breathed life into the Word. (2 Timothy 3:16). Therefore, the Word is said to be God-breathed and God-inspired. It is life-giving and has the power to resurrect and revive anyone who is spiritually dead.

John tells us that *"In the beginning was the Word, and the Word was with God, and the Word was God. . .and the Word became flesh and dwelt among us. . ."* (John 1:1, 14). Jesus is the Word become flesh, and He has provided us a perfect example of how to live life abundantly through God's Word.

The source of all breath, all life, comes from God. Adam did not come alive until God breathed life into him (Genesis 2:7), and it is the same with you. Rely on God for every breath you take—your life depends on it. Similarly, you must depend on God for your spiritual breath. If you desire to live life fully, learn to breathe spiritually.

INTRODUCTION

A WAKE-UP CALL

Have you ever driven home from work and, once you arrived, didn't remember anything about the journey? It happens all the time. I remember driving home from work one day when one of my sisters called and asked me to pick up my nephew. My sister, Daphne, was working late that evening and would not make it to the after-school program in time to pick up her son. I told her that I would be glad to do it.

Later that evening, after being home for a while, my phone rang. When I looked at the caller id, my heart sank. *Oh, my gosh. I forgot to pick up my nephew!* After talking with my sister, I realized that in my autopilot state of mind, I had driven straight home like I did every day. **If we want to experience the abundant life God has waiting for us, we have to come out of autopilot and take back the wheel of our lives.**

I remember a time when I was a child, waking up one morning to my sisters teasing me about my missing a trip to our local city's amusement park the night before. They told me that they had gone to Astroworld, but they didn't take me because I had been asleep and no one could wake me. I thought for sure they were making it all up, but when they showed me the big, round, colorful lollipops that we only got at Astroworld, I took off running to my mother to see if it was true.

My heart sank when she confirmed their story. She scolded them for not bringing back a lollipop for me, but I still wanted to know how they could have gone without me. Mom said they just couldn't wake me, so she stayed home while our father took my sisters to the park. I was devastated and felt so cheated.

How could they not wake me up? *They didn't try hard enough*, I told myself. All they needed to do was shake me harder.

What about you? What is it going to take to shake you out of this unconscious state and wake you up to the abundant life that awaits you? I don't know about you, but I don't want to miss out on the best that life has to offer because I've been asleep at the wheel of my life. **It's time to do whatever it takes to wake yourself up and get fully engaged in your life.**

I pray that this book will serve as your wake-up call. You see, the enemy counts on you being asleep. While you're not looking, he sends in his evil angels to steal your hope, joy, and peace. You may have met some of them.

Are you familiar with Ms. Anger? She likes to steal your joy. Ms. Worrier likes to steal your peace. Ms. Procrastinator likes to keep you from making progress. Then there is Ms. Ungrateful—she likes to keep you in a state of discontent. We'll get familiar with these thieving spirits, and more, as we take this journey together. For now, just become consciously aware that they want to steal the abundant life you seek.

IS SOMETHING BLOCKING THE FLOW OF GOD'S INSPIRED WORD INTO YOUR LIFE?

I was raised in the church and as a child, I accepted Christ. I am keenly aware of the promises of God, yet, if I am honest, I find myself continually struggling to hold on to the peace, hope, and joy that I know is available to me. As Christians, we read the Word, recite the Word, sing the Word, shout the Word, even dance to the Word. But the more revealing question is: *are we walking in the Word in our daily lives?* I can easily relate to Paul

INTRODUCTION

when he says, "what I want to do, I don't do, and what I don't want to do, I do." (Romans 7:15). Does this describe you, too?

So how do you know if something is blocking the flow of God's inspired Word into your life? Here are a few signs:

- You feel joy only when everything is going your way.
- The moment you experience a setback, your peace goes with the wind.
- You struggle with negative thoughts that seem to consume you.
- You have many goals, but you lack the confidence and energy to pursue them.
- You procrastinate more than you make progress.
- You know that you were created for more, but you don't know how to be more.
- You've buried and forgotten your "real" dreams.
- Others see more in you than you see in yourself.
- You believe that because of your past, it's not possible to have a great future.
- You have become complacent and settled for a life that is far less than your best.
- You do things to sabotage your own success.

- You believe that attaining more wealth, job status, or material possessions will make you happier.

- You believe that there is not enough to go around (enough money, enough jobs, etc.).

- You have gifts and talents that you have not fully tapped.

- You feel that you are just "going through the motions." Life is routine, and you are on autopilot.

- You feel trapped, like you don't have room to breathe.

These are real struggles that Christians face every day. But how do you overcome them so you can start living the joyful, fulfilling life you were created to live? In order to receive all that God has available for you, you must submit to the process of becoming all He created you to be. When you inhale, you receive the oxygen that fuels your body and allows it to carry out its functions.

Compare that to spiritual breathing. When we spiritually inhale, we are inspired with God's Word. We inhale all that is God, all that is good. With each breath you take, you will become more of the person God created you to be. You will be in the position to live a richer, fuller, more authentic life infused with love, joy, and peace. You will be energized and inspired to relentlessly pursue your purpose with a passion.

As the Word becomes alive in you, you will have a new lease on life and will be empowered to live life more fully. But breathing is a two-part process. The complete respiration process allows

INTRODUCTION

you to exchange toxins that you don't need for the oxygen that you do need. And after the inspiration must come expiration.

During expiration, we breathe out, releasing carbon dioxide and other toxic wastes from our body. In this same way, we must learn to exhale spiritually, releasing the emotional and mental toxins that pollute our lives. We must let go of anger, fear, unforgiveness, doubt, worry, and every negative emotion and mindset that keeps us from becoming all we were meant to be.

Mastering the art of spiritual breathing will allow you to exchange toxic emotions and mindsets for more healthy ones that promote your well-being: hatred will be exchanged for love; fear will be replaced with courage; and peace will move into space once occupied by worry and anxiety. As you release these negative toxins from your life, you open up a pathway and create space to receive all that God has for you.

The more we practice the art of spiritual breathing, the more natural and automatic it will become. Eventually, it should become as natural as what our lungs do for us every day. As we breathe spiritually, we will be emptied of the spiritual toxins that break us down, and in turn be filled with the spiritual oxygen that builds us up.

As you learn to depend upon God for your every breath—both physically and spiritually—you will begin to develop a deeper, more intimate relationship with Him. With each breath you take, you will become more alive and awakened to who you really are. Each breath renews, revives, rejuvenates, and restores your soul. You will become awakened to the limitless possibilities and potential for your life.

WHAT MORE ARE YOU SEARCHING FOR?

Before you embark on this journey, think about this question: "What more are you searching for?" Are you seeking more peace, more love, more hope, or more joy? What about more confidence, more courage, or more strength? Could you use more wisdom, more freedom, and more authenticity? How about more balance, more purpose, and more passion?

God has everything you need and more! This book is about flowing and growing into your greatness and becoming more and more of who God created you to be, one breath at a time. If you will give God your "less than," He'll give you His "more than." He will shape, make, and mold you into more than you ever imagined you could be. Are you ready to get to your *more*? Are you ready to grow your wings and flow into your greatness? Take a moment to pause and take a deep breath…

Now let's flow and grow together as we enter the process of becoming more.

INSPIRATION 1:
Inhale Abundance

Embracing All That Is Available to You

> *Now unto him that is able to do exceeding abundantly above all that we ask or think, according to the power that worketh in us.*
> (EPHESIANS 3:20 KJV)

In this chapter, we will begin to flow and grow with God's inspired Word on **abundance**. Everything that you need has already been made available to you. Before God created Man, He saw to it that everything Man would need was already available to him. He created the sun and the moon, the oceans and land, trees and animals. By the time Man showed up to the universe, there was nothing to do besides enjoy and embrace everything that was already available to him.

Today, there's a prevailing mentality that there's not enough—that we all have to fight and compete for the limited resources available. I think of the game of musical chairs—there's always one less seat than there are participants. Everyone circles around the chairs like vultures, ready to devour anyone who gets in their way. They're not free to simply enjoy the music because their sole focus is on making sure they end up with a seat. When the music stops, it really gets ugly—there's

INSPIRATION 1: INHALE ABUNDANCE

knocking and pushing and shoving. The most aggressive players are the ones who end up successfully landing in a chair.

Unfortunately, we see this game being played out in life today. Many of us are not able to simply enjoy our lives because we're too focused on competing for those perceived limited resources. Many believe that they must knock others down in order to pull themselves up.

There is a mindset that says, "in order for me to get mines, you can't get yours." Society convinces us that there are not enough opportunities, jobs, money, and (particularly for African American women) not enough men to go around. So if you want to get yours, you must sabotage the success of others.

This lack mentality that is plaguing our society is unhealthy and unfruitful. Through the TV, radio, magazines, billboards and the Internet, advertisers bombard us with messages that say, "in order to *be* more, we must *get* more." They convince us that we can't possibly be happy until we buy their product—because it will make us more beautiful, more respected, more important, more joyful, or more intelligent.

In our desperate pursuit to get more, we end up sacrificing our morals and values. We adopt an "I'll do whatever it takes" mentality and find ourselves doing things that we know are outside of God's will as we try to get what we want. But even after we fill up our lives with the things we were pursuing, there's still a void. We still feel empty and unfulfilled. The cycle then repeats itself and we search for more things to complete us.

SEEK GOD FIRST

Abundance is about being fulfilled, but you will never obtain that feeling of being whole and complete as long as you are seeking after the things of this world. We are to seek first the Kingdom of God and all other things will follow. (see Mathew 6:33)

God wants to be first on your list of the things you seek. He wants you to thirst and hunger after Him. God wants you to develop a deep, intimate relationship with Him. If you trust God, He promises to provide all your needs and then some. You don't have to worry about competing to get yours. What God has for you is for you and you alone.

I believe that God has a promised land for each one of us. Your land of promise looks different from mine. Your promised land is that place that God has shown you in your vision. This is the place that is overflowing with milk and honey. There is no lack in this land. When you get in this place in life, you will be perfectly positioned to receive all that God has for you.

Looking back on the children of Israel, we see how God delivered them from Egypt. He promised to take them to their promised land in Canaan, but to get there, He led them through the wilderness. They didn't understand it and they fought it, whined, and complained every step of the way. But God took them through the wilderness to prepare them for their promised land. They did not yet have the character to appreciate that promised land. You see, God had taken them out of Egypt, but now He had to take Egypt out of them! They still had an Egypt mentality. They had to learn to trust God and depend on *Him* for their every need.

INSPIRATION 1: INHALE ABUNDANCE

As Christians, we have been delivered from Egypt—from the penalty of sin. Through God's grace, we are promised a life in Eternity. But God also wants us to start enjoying the abundant life right here on earth. Before God can lead you into the abundance that He has available for you, He needs to make and shape you into who He created you to be.

The key to getting all that God has for you is becoming all that He created you to be. As you move closer to *being* who God created you to *be*, you'll move closer to *doing* what God created you to *do*. We'll discuss purpose and passion in greater detail later, but just know that God wants you to pursue your purpose with a passion.

Before you can do so, though, you must develop the character needed to get the job done. It is on your unique path to purpose that you will find your most abundant opportunities. God has uniquely gifted and equipped you for His divine purposes. You will find God's favor most abundantly on the path that He specifically created for you.

If you're following someone else's path, you'll miss your blessings. When you're operating outside of God's will for your life, you'll find yourself desperately chasing down blessings, trying to make things happen that are not of God's will. When you get on the path that is uniquely yours, you won't have to chase the blessings down—they will chase *you* down!

MAKE ROOM TO RECEIVE

When you are working within God's will, you won't have room enough to receive all the blessings that He has for you. This is why we must clear the space and make room to receive the things of God. It seems that we are continually focused on what we can *get*, but we need to also focus on what we need to *get rid of*. What do you need to let go of in order to make room to receive from God?

We often like to hold on to things that are comfortable and familiar, even if they are useless to us now. You need to continually clear out the clutter in your closets, drawers, and every area of your home to make room for something new. If your closets are packed to capacity with old clothes that you no longer wear, how can you bring in a fresh new wardrobe? Clear out the clutter and be willing to let go of anything that no longer serves a purpose in your life.

Spiritually speaking, you must examine every mindset and emotion that you are clinging to. As we go through this book, we'll uncover some of the negative thought patterns and self-sabotaging behaviors that we need to let go of. Toxic spirits like anger, fear, procrastination, worry, bitterness, discontent, and low self-esteem only serve to hold us back and keep us from the abundant life we deserve to live.

GOD HAS EVERYTHING YOU NEED

John 10:10 KJV tells us, "The thief cometh not, but for to steal, and to kill, and to destroy: I am come that they might have life, and that they might have it more abundantly."

Jesus came to give life and to give it to the full. In God, you will find an unlimited supply of love, joy, hope, peace, and everything necessary to make your life richer and more enjoyable. Let's take oxygen as an example. The universe holds all the oxygen you need and more. You are not competing with anyone else to get your share of this vital resource—it is abundantly available to you.

If you're not getting the oxygen you need, it's because you have shut yourself off from receiving it. Let's demonstrate that right now. Stop for a moment and focus on your breath. Now stop breathing. Hold your breath for as long as you can. How long did you last? I can't even make it to a minute. The time that you were without oxygen was your choice. It was not because the oxygen was not readily available; it was because you *chose* not to open up and receive it.

I've discovered that we often like to selectively focus on the words in Scriptures that appeal to us, but it's important to look at *all* of the words to get the full meaning. If God has made everything abundantly available to us, why, then, are we not receiving it? To find the answer to that question, let's look back at John 10:10. This verse tells us that although Jesus came to give life abundantly, the enemy came to steal, kill, and destroy.

In other words, the enemy is working to undo everything that Jesus came to do—the enemy wants to kill your hopes and dreams and he aims to rob you of your joy, hope, and peace. Everything that God is trying to give to you, the enemy is trying to take from you. God wants to breathe life into you, but the enemy wants to suck the life out of you!

THE SPIRITUAL BATTLE FOR YOUR LIFE

If you have not realized it yet, there is a spiritual war going on here and what's up for grabs is your life. The Bible tells us that "our struggle is not against flesh and blood, but against the rulers, against the authorities, against the powers of this dark world and against the spiritual forces of evil in the heavenly realms." (see Ephesians 6:12)

Satan does not work alone. He has an army of evil angels that he deploys on his behalf. Your fight is not with your spouse, your children, your boss, and those you believe are out to get you. The real battle is happening in the spiritual realm, with evil forces that you can't even see.

AUTHENTIC ABUNDANCE

In our pursuit of the abundant life, we must be careful about what we are pursuing. God promises to supply all of our needs according to His riches and glory (see Philippians 4:19). He did not promise to make you a millionaire, and anyone who tells you that is trying to deceive you. If God blesses you with great wealth, that's wonderful. Money is not evil; it is putting the *pursuit* of money—or any other worldly thing—ahead of the pursuit of a real relationship with God that will get you into trouble. Remember, our first priority should be an intimate relationship with God. "You shall have no other gods before Me." (Exodus 20:3)

Authentic abundance is about so much more than money. In fact, the most valuable things that God has to offer are priceless and no amount of money can be used to buy them. God offers an abundance of health, hope, grace, peace, love, joy…and so much more.

All of the money in the world won't buy you peace of mind. The type of peace that I'm after is the peace that surpasses all understanding. I want the type of joy that the world didn't give and the world can't take away. I want to be like Paul and be content regardless of my circumstances (see Philippians 4:11). Money and material possessions will come and go, but if you have an abundance of peace, you'll be able to find joy through it all.

PROVISION FOR THE VISION

Please don't misunderstand me. You should strive to be as successful as you can be, but never at the cost of your relationship with God. I believe that God has a vision for each one of us, and we'll discuss this in greater detail in another chapter.

For now, just know that God promises to make provision for the vision. Whatever plan God has for your life, He will make provision for it. He will provide you with what you need to fulfill your purpose and make your dream become a reality.

What you need in order to accomplish your goals may be far different from what I need to complete mine. If your vision entails a worldwide ministry, you'll need far greater resources than if it is to minister to your local community. Neither goal is more important than the other—each simply requires a different set of resources. Trust that God will supply you with all you need, and more, to accomplish the vision He has entrusted in you.

I pray that you get it into your spirit that God wants the best for you. He wants to bless you beyond your wildest imaginations. Our God is without limits, and the possibilities and potential for your life are unlimited when you trust in Him. In order to receive all that is available to you, you must release some things and create the space to receive. Any toxic mindset and emotion that prevents you from receiving all that God has to offer must

EMBRACING ALL THAT IS AVAILABLE TO YOU

be purged from your life. Like the oxygen we breathe so freely, God is waiting to release a free flow of hope, love, joy, and peace into your life. We must do what is necessary to clear the way to receive it.

If Ms. Lack is occupying space in your life, let her know that her time has expired. She is no longer welcomed in your world. It is time to show her the exit door. As you breathe out *lack*, you'll begin to breathe in *abundance* and all that God has to offer. You are closer to it than you may believe. *Just Breathe.* Your abundant life is just a breath away.

INSPIRATION 2:
Inhale Gratitude

Cultivating an Attitude of Thankfulness

Give thanks in all circumstances, for this is God's will for you in Christ Jesus.
(Thessalonians 5:18)

In this chapter, we will begin to flow and grow with God's inspired Word on **gratitude**. Each morning when I wake up, I silently recite this prayer, *Thank you God for waking me up this morning to see a brand new day. Thank you for today, because today is the present and the present is a gift.* Waking up with an attitude of gratitude has really changed my perspective.

I did not always embrace the new day this way. In the past, I would moan when the alarm clock sounded and I began my "I don't want to get up" mantra. After fighting it for as long as I could, I would drag myself out of bed, still having an attitude that I had to get up and go to a job that I didn't want to go to. Sound familiar?

Shifting your perspective and focusing on the blessing of a new day is a much better way to start your day. Now, I bounce out of bed with new energy, ready to tackle the day ahead. I realize that not everyone who went to sleep last night woke up this morning, so I should simply be grateful. God has chosen to continue to breathe life into me and for that alone, I am grateful.

COUNT UP YOUR BLESSINGS

In the previous chapter, we focused on inhaling abundance. Abundance is more about your attitude and mindset than anything else. You will never experience authentic abundance if you are only able to see what is wrong and missing in your life. Awaken to the wonderful blessings already present in this moment in time.

Consider it right now. What do you have to be thankful for in this very moment? Why don't you start with your breath and work your way out from there. Our breath is probably the most precious gift we have, yet we often overlook it. It is what connects us to God. It is life, and without it we cease to exist. Thank God for every breath you take. Thank God for His breathed Word that keeps you spiritually alive and thriving.

What about your health and strength? Even if you are not in the best of health, you are still here, so thank God for that and for the healing that you know is coming. Be thankful for your beautiful children, even if they do not always do what you wish. Even when you are experiencing trials and tribulations, be thankful that God is there to pull you through.

Be thankful for every little detail. Do not skip over any of your blessings. I love taking hot bubble baths, so I am grateful for hot water. As I am typing right now, I am grateful for my computer, the use of my hands, and my sight. I am on a mini-retreat, sitting on a balcony which overlooks a beautiful lake. I am thankful for the clear blue sky and the warmth of the sun hitting my back. I appreciate the sound of chirping birds and the sight of those in flight gracing the skyline. I love water—the feel of it, the sound of it, the sight of it. I am grateful for the calm, flowing water before me because it soothes my soul. Do you get the idea? Be grateful!

LEARN TO BE CONTENT

Purposefully cultivate an attitude of gratefulness. It is much easier to be ungrateful and focus on what you do not have or what you perceive as missing and lacking in your life. When you continually focus on what you do not have, you set yourself up to be miserable and unhappy. This spirit of ungratefulness is called discontent.

Ms. Discontent convinces you that you cannot be happy until you get everything you want and everything goes your way. When you get the new job, new house, new car, and new relationship, *then* you can be happy. When you lose the weight, start your business, or get out of debt, *then* you will have something to celebrate. Until then, Ms. Discontent wants you to be bitter and unhappy. If you are not in perfect health, have the perfect job, or the perfect relationship, "What do you have to be thankful for?" she asks you. If you allow Ms. Discontent to continue to have her way, you will miss out on the many blessings already abundantly present in your life.

Become like Paul and learn to be content no matter the circumstances (see Philippians 4:11). Not everything will always go your way. Life is full of challenges and obstacles. There is always going to be something that you want to change in your life. If change is in your control, then by all means, work towards making the change. But in the meantime, be content right where you are. When you are taking a long road trip to your favorite destination, don't wait until you get there to start enjoying your vacation. Learn to enjoy the journey along the way. Do not put off being happy until you accomplish your goals; be thankful for the entire process.

TAKE STOCK OF WHAT IS LEFT

Over the past decade, I have gone through three major industry downturns. I was working for an energy company during the oil and gas industry downturn back in 2002. The company where I was working came tumbling down within a year after the infamous Enron scandal. I was one of the hundreds of workers sent home with only a box of my belongings and a wiped out retirement account.

Within a year, I shifted into the home construction industry. After about five years of building up my savings again, I was victim to another industry downturn—the banking and housing industry collapse that led the Great Recession back in 2008. Again, I was sent home with a box in my hand and a grossly deflated retirement account.

Then I switched to what was supposed to be a stable career during that time—I became a teacher. After teaching for a couple of years, I was laid off in 2011, along with several other Texas teachers, due to a state budget crisis.

I am a single mother with a small son to provide for. I could have become bitter very easily. But I had a choice to make: either I could sit around and be angry at the world and God for allowing me to yet again be in this position, or I could be grateful for what I still had.

Yes, I had lost yet another job and my source of income. I had lost thousands of dollars in savings. The market was flooded with other job seekers and many corporations were shedding jobs rather than creating them. But instead of licking my wounds and whining about what I had lost, I decided to focus on what I had left: first and foremost, I had my precious son; I had my health and strength plus family and friends to support me; I had my home and reliable transportation; and, because I was financially wise when I was earning an income, I had a good cushion of emergency savings outside of the stock market.

Yes, I had lost a lot, but I was also left with a lot. And whatever had been taken away, I trusted God to restore in His timing. This is the type of attitude that we must have in life. I used those situations to make me better, not bitter. I know that I am stronger today because of the trials I've endured.

When you experience great loss in your life, turn from what has been lost and take stock of what is left. Then move forward and work with what you've got. You have more than you realize, and God is the Master of taking what you have and multiplying it into more. I never missed a mortgage or car payment and my bills were paid on time. God took me through those situations with ease. I believe that it was because I kept a positive and grateful attitude and relied on God to provide.

FINDING PEACE IN THE STORM

Back in 2008, Hurricane Ike came across the Galveston, Texas, shores, which is about forty-five miles from where I live. As the storm approached and the forecast predicted it to strengthen, my family decided at the last minute to pack a few things and head north to Dallas to escape its impact. As we were leaving

INSPIRATION 2: INHALE GRATITUDE

out of the house, my then-seven-year-old son, Donnie, said, "Momma, when we get back home, you are going to look at this mess and say, *oh my gosh,* and then pass out." I laughed at him and told him that our home should be fine. We were far inland in the city of Houston. We just did not want to stay home and deal with the high winds, no water, and no electricity.

After the storm passed, and the roads were clear enough, we headed home. Upon opening the door to my home, I was glad to see that everything appeared to be intact. As I walked around downstairs, I noticed that a rug in the bathroom was wet; I assumed there was some kind of leak from the toilet. I then walked upstairs and my jaw dropped—the ceiling had caved in and insulation from the attic was all over the place. My beautiful wooden floors and furniture were all soaked and ruined.

My breath was taken away. I was shocked, but I quickly composed myself and got in gear for what was a long road to restoring my home. I could have been angry, devastated or depressed about the situation, but instead I thanked God that my son and I were safely away in Dallas when the storm blew through and destroyed part of our home. The home could be repaired. All that mattered was that we were okay.

In the end, the insurance money paid out as it should, and I ended up with a remodeled home. My son said, "Momma, two of my predictions came true. The house was messed up and you said, *oh my gosh*...but you didn't pass out." It still amazes me to this day that he received a vision of what was to come. But I did not pass out because I decided to focus on what I had left instead of what I had lost. I had my son and we both had our health and strength, and that is all that mattered. Material things will come and go, but choose to hold on to your joy and peace in the midst of it all.

PRAISE HIM THROUGH IT ALL

And we know that in all things God works for the good of those who love him, who have been called according to his purpose.
(Romans 8:28)

Please get this down in your spirit. God has a way of working things out for your good if you trust Him to do so. In the meantime, praise Him as if it were already done. The Book of Psalms is saturated with thanksgivings to God:

Praise the Lord. Give thanks to the Lord, for he is good; his love endures forever.
(Psalms 106:1)

I will bless the LORD at all times: his praise shall continually be in my mouth.
(Psalms 34:1 KJV)

Praise lifts your spirit and gives you the energy that you need to keep on fighting the good fight of faith. It soothes your soul and heals your heart. I know this is difficult to do when it seems that life has dealt you a devastating blow.

To this day, I do not understand why God allowed my sister, Andrea, to be taken away from my family so soon. I am sure that I will never comprehend it. But I have learned to be grateful for the time God blessed us with her presence and for the cherished memories that I now hold dear to my heart.

ARE YOU ASKING THE RIGHT QUESTION?

When we experience difficulties in our lives, we may find ourselves asking God why. "Why did you allow this to happen to me?" "Why are you allowing me to experience so much pain?" There is nothing wrong with questioning God, but we must learn to ask the right type of questions. Asking God "why" will only frustrate you because you are likely to not receive an answer that meets your satisfaction.

The mysteries of this world belong to God. There are simply things that we will never understand while we are in this world. We may never fully comprehend why God allows us to go through certain things. Our small minds cannot begin to process on God's level.

May I suggest that instead of asking God *why*, ask Him *how*, *what*, and *where*. How can I grow from this situation, God? What do you want me to learn from this circumstance? Where do you want me to go in my life from here? Asking these types of questions sets you up to learn, grow, and become stronger from what you have endured. It enables you to position yourself to become a *better* you instead of a *bitter* you.

> *I don't know what you have gone through, what you're currently going through, or what lies ahead for you, but I pray that you are able to find it in your spirit to praise God, regardless of your circumstances. Praise Him in the good times and bad. Know that He will never leave you nor forsake you.*
> (DEUTERONOMY 31:6)

CULTIVATING AN ATTITUDE OF THANKFULNESS

As you exhale to release ungratefulness and discontent, you will create the space to begin cultivating a new joyful life of gratitude. You are closer to it than you may believe. Just breathe. Your life of thanksgiving and gratefulness is just a breath away.

INSPIRATION 3:
Inhale Grace

Accepting God's Unlimited Favor

> *For it is by grace you have been saved, through faith--*
> *and this not from yourselves, it is the gift of God.*
> (EPHESIANS 2:8)

In the previous chapter, we worked on inhaling and experiencing gratitude toward God. In this chapter, we will begin to flow and grow with God's inspired Word on **grace**.

Before we travel much further in this spiritual journey, I want you to inhale God's grace deep down in your spirit. *Inspired To Be More* is about becoming a grace-filled, better you. This process of *becoming* requires transformation and change, but Satan does not want you to change. He employs the twin spirits, Ms. Guilt and Ms. Shame, to keep you in your current condition, because he knows that guilt and shame never lead to change. If he can keep you dwelling in guilt and shame over your shortcomings, he can keep you from making any real progress towards becoming a better you.

If you continuously beat yourself down because of your mistakes, you lack the confidence needed to move forward boldly into the abundant life God called you to live. This is why it is so important that you come to fully understand God's

INSPIRATION 3: INHALE GRACE

amazing grace. It is His grace that saved you and is continuing to keep you to this day.

If you desire to become all that God created you to be, learn how to grow in His grace. Grace is defined as God's unmerited, or undeserved, favor toward sinners. In order to fully appreciate grace, we must look back to the beginning of time to understand why we need it.

> *The LORD God formed the man from the dust of the ground and breathed into his nostrils the breath of life, and the man became a living being.*
> (GENESIS 2:7)

Up until this point, God had brought all of His creations into existence by His spoken Word. (See Genesis 1:3 where He said, "Let there be light," and there was light.) But when God created Man, He chose to do so in a more intimate way. He formed Man and breathed His breath of life into Him. He invested His own image and likeness into His human creation (see Genesis 1:26).

It is clear that God intended to have an intimate relationship with Man. God intended for us to worship and honor Him in His glory.

Instead, falling into Satan's temptation, Man sinned against God's commandment and ate from the forbidden Tree of the Knowledge of Good and Evil.

This blatant sin against God marked the beginning of Man's separation from God. Sin severed our relationship with God and broke our fellowship with Him. Man was expelled from the Garden of Eden and began to suffer the consequences of his actions. The sentence for sinning against God was spiritual death and Man could do nothing to save himself. (Genesis 2:17)

THE PERFECT SACRIFICE

God could have chosen to destroy all of mankind. But although He hated sin, He loved us more. Out of His unwavering love for us, He devised a plan to save us all. That perfect plan, The Perfect Sacrifice, was His precious Son, Jesus Christ. Only Christ, who lived on earth as a man free from sin, could be offered up to atone for our transgressions.

When Jesus died on the cross, His last words were, "It is finished." (See John 19:30) God's amazing plan of salvation for mankind was complete. God accepted the Perfect Sacrifice of His Son as final payment in full for our sins.

Now, anyone who believes in Jesus Christ and accepts Him as Lord and Savior and repents of sin will be restored into a right relationship with God. This amazing act of love and mercy releases those who believe in Him from the eternal death penalty of sin. This is God's saving grace.

> *But because of His great love for us, God, who is rich in mercy, made us alive with Christ even when we were dead in transgressions—it is by grace you have been saved.*
> (Ephesians 2:4-5)

We were once spiritually dead but God's grace saved us and made us alive again. We were dead in our spirit, but God quickened us and breathed a fresh breath of new life into our spirit.

Now, we are alive to God and we live, breathe, and move in Him.

In the same way that God resurrected Jesus from the dead, He has brought us back to life to live for His purposes. The Spirit of God has taken up residence in us and we now have the power to live life fully. God wants to resurrect your dreams, revive your passions, restore your soul, and renew your spirit. By the grace of God, you can become all He created you to be and do all He created you to do.

GRACE TO GROW

God's grace does not end with your salvation—your sanctification is of great interest to Him as well. God not only wants to save you, He wants to change you to become what He created you to be—sanctification is that process. It is only through God's grace that you are able to grow and walk in the works He has prepared for you.

> *For we are God's workmanship, created in Christ Jesus to do good works, which God prepared in advance for us to do.*
> (EPHESIANS 2:10)

God gives you the grace to grow fully into who He created you to be so you can do what He has created you to do. But if you don't accept that grace, you'll miss out on the opportunity to fulfill your purpose and glorify God. When you make mistakes and poor choices, the accuser (Satan) may convince you that you've blown it. He tries to get you to believe that you've messed up so badly that God cannot use you. That condemning voice repeatedly reminds you of every law you've broken and every misstep you've made. He leads you to believe that because of your failures, you are no longer useful to God. This may weigh you down with guilt and shame, but realize that the voice you are hearing is *not* the voice of God.

When you live in opposition to God's will for your life, the Holy Spirit will convict you. He convicts you so He can convince you to change—but He does not condemn you. Condemnation only leads to guilt and shame, and those toxic emotions never lead to change.

When you are wallowing in guilt and shame, you begin to have a "pity party." Self-pity is really self-centeredness—the focus is on you. You are consumed with thoughts of how badly you messed things up. Instead, take your focus off yourself and put it on God. Instead of focusing on what you did to mess things up, focus on what He did to clean up your mess.

Instead of concentrating on how bad you think you are, meditate on how good you know God is. Instead of dwelling on your imperfections, remember the Perfect Sacrifice that was made for your life. Instead of focusing on the debt you owe, focus on the price Jesus has already paid.

LEAVE THE PAST BEHIND

You may have made poor choices and opened the doors to trouble in your life, but know that God's mercy is greater than your mistakes. Declare that you will not live with guilt. God knows you are not perfect—that's why He devised the perfect plan to save you from yourself. When the Holy Spirit convicts you of your wrongdoing, be quick to repent, accept God's forgiveness, and move on.

INSPIRATION 3: INHALE GRACE

God not only forgives, He forgets. He does not remind you of your mistakes every opportunity He gets, the way people often do. Instead, He redeems and restores you into a right relationship with Him. He gives you a fresh new start and releases you from your past.

Learn to get spiritual amnesia. Stop re-living your past and keeping it alive. God is trying to do a new thing in you, but you keep holding on to the old. You must exhale and release the carbon dioxide before you can inhale a fresh new breath of oxygen. Let go of your old mistakes and shortcomings, and move forward into what God has for you now. Accept God's mercy and grow in His grace.

Don't let your past hinder what God has called you to do. Others need what God has put in you—they need you to shine your light on them. God will use what you have been through to minister to others, but you can't help others until you first accept God's help for your own life. God has already given you everything you need to live the abundant life you were created to live. When you accepted Him as your Savior, He bestowed many spiritual blessing upon you.

FORGIVE AND FORGET

One of the things that can hinder you from fully receiving God's grace is an inability to extend forgiveness to others. When Jesus taught the disciples how to pray, He made forgiveness the cornerstone of their relationship with God. If you hope to receive God's mercy in your own circumstances, you must first be willing to forgive those who have wronged you (see Luke 11:4). When you refuse to forgive others, it shows that you do not fully grasp your own desperate need to be forgiven.

ACCEPTING GOD'S UNLIMITED FAVOR

> *This righteousness from God comes through faith in Jesus Christ to all who believe. There is no difference, for all have sinned and fall short of the glory of God.*
> (Romans 3:22-23)

We are made righteous and restored to a right relationship with God only through our faith in Christ. It is not because we are so good; it is because He is so good. It is only by the grace of God that we are able to enter into God's Holy presence. We have done nothing to deserve God's favor.

We must never forget the dead state that we were in when we were separated from God and lost in our sin. As long as we live in this earthen, broken vessel, we will continue to fall short and need God's mercy. God commands us to extend this same mercy to others. Like God, we must learn to hate the sin but love the sinner.

Forgiveness is not always easy. While some offenses may be easily overlooked, others are so painful that you may feel that you could never forgive, let alone forget. You may have been deeply wounded, disrespected, violated, or mistreated by someone.

Life presents us with many opportunities to forgive: from the person who cut you off on the road and the man who walked out leaving you to raise your kids alone, to the person who was supposed to be your friend but violated your trust, and the boss who passed you up for a promotion you deserved.

Letting go of these offenses is not easy, but it *is* necessary. Forgiveness is not only for the other person—it is more for you. The person who offended you may have already forgotten

INSPIRATION 3: INHALE GRACE

it, has gone on to living life and is happy as can be. Meanwhile, you are bound by your bitterness and can't break free to enjoy your life. When you hold on to the spirit of unforgiveness, you harbor anger inside of you. You're hurting yourself, not the other person. Holding on to unforgiveness can even manifest itself as serious health issues.

When you don't forgive, you block your own blessings and hinder the free flow of God's grace into your life. You're not able to inhale the joy and peace that God is breathing into your spirit. Release the anger and bitterness that has you bound.

This does not mean that you are giving the other person a free pass to hurt you—you are freeing yourself from past hurt and pain. Vengeance does not belong to you; it belongs to God alone. God will right your wrongs. Be quick to forgive, forget, and free your soul.

For those issues too difficult to let go, pray and ask God for His power to release them. The same power that was called upon to redeem your soul is the same power that is living in you today. You have the power to forgive and forget with God's grace. If you hope to become a better you, let go of all bitterness and baggage holding you back from becoming all God created you to be.

GROW IN HIS GRACE

> *But by the grace of God I am what I am, and his grace to me was not without effect. No, I worked harder than all of them—yet not I, but the grace of God that was with me.*
> (1 CORINTHIANS 15:10)

Paul was humbly acknowledging that all he had accomplished was owed to God. He was not competent and capable of doing anything outside of God; it was only because of the grace of God upon His life that he accomplished so much.

True humility does not require that you consider yourself worthless. It's about you recognizing God's work in you and His hand of grace and mercy upon your life. You can only go so far in your own natural abilities, but with God's grace, you can grow fully into who He created you to be.

God created you to be so much more than you are living and experiencing right now. He has great things in store for you. If you will accept His favor and grow in His grace, you will become more than you ever imagined you could be.

God's grace goes beyond unmerited favor. It is the power of the Holy Spirit imparted to you to do with ease what you could not do by yourself. You cannot change yourself. Apart from God, you do not have the power to overcome your strongholds and shortcomings. But with His mercy, you can conquer your anger, love those who mistreat you, and hold on to your peace in the midst of life's storms. By the grace of God, you can be freed from low self-esteem, hopelessness, hatred, and every negative spirit that threatens to keep you from God's promises.

As you exhale to release guilt, shame, and unforgiveness, you will open up the floodgates to allow God's free flow of grace to enter into your life. You are closer to it than you may believe. Just breathe. Your life of grace and favor is just a breath away.

INSPIRATION 4:
Inhale Love

Embracing God's Unlimited Affection for You

For God so loved the world that He gave His one and only Son, that whoever believes in Him shall not perish but have eternal life.
(JOHN 3:16)

In the previous chapter, we worked on inhaling and receiving God's grace. In this chapter, we will begin to flow and grow with God's inspired Word on **love**.

You may be wondering why God chose to have mercy on us and save us when we did not deserve to be saved. Why would God sacrifice His precious Son, who perfectly kept the law, for people who disregarded the law? Why would He allow His only Son to suffer so greatly and endure such pain? Why did God choose to give us eternal life, instead of allowing the true sentence of death that we deserved to be carried out? The answer to these questions can be found in the verse below:

This is how God showed His love among us: He sent His one and only Son into the world that we might live through Him.
(1 JOHN 4:9)

INSPIRATION 4: INHALE LOVE

God made such a great sacrifice for us because He loves us so much. He hated the sin that separated us from Him, but He loved us more. Instead of destroying us as He could have, He chose to rescue us and restore us into a right relationship with Him. It is difficult to grasp this level of love because it is not in our nature to love this way.

THE WORLD'S WAY VS. GOD'S WAY

The world's way of love is far different from God's way. The world's system of love is complicated, because we make it complicated. But God's love is simple. The world's system of love says, "I'll love you if you do this and that." God's system of love says, "I'll love you."

There are no if's, and's, or but's about it—God loves you regardless of what you do or don't do. The world's system of love says, "If you stop doing this or that, I will stop loving you." God's system of love says, "There is nothing you can do to stop Me from loving you." Do you grasp the difference? God's love is perfect and unconditional. You don't have to do anything to earn or keep it, because it is bestowed upon you freely and abundantly. There is no better and greater love than the love of God.

The world's love is *reactionary*; it is in response to what someone does or does not do. God's love is *initiated*; it is not in response to anything you do or do not do. God did not wait until we got our collective acts together and started obeying His law perfectly before He decided to love us. He did not say, "If you obey me and believe in my Son, then I will save you." He took the initiative to lavish us with His love while we were still sinners and going about our business with no regard to His law.

> *Very rarely will anyone die for a righteous man, though for a good man someone might possibly dare to die. But God demonstrates his own love for us in this: While we were still sinners, Christ died for us.*
> (Romans 5:7-8)

It's difficult enough to conceive dying for a person who has done you no harm; can you imagine sacrificing your life for a person who is not righteous and deserves the sentence of death? Yet this is exactly what Jesus did for us. He gave His life so we may live. We are not worthy of God's sacrificial love, but He gives it to us freely.

God's love is far different from the love we express to each other. His love is referred to as *agape* love. The essence of *agape* love is self-sacrifice. There is no greater sacrifice than that of God giving up His Son's life to save mankind.

The Lord's love is not sentimental and based on feelings that come and go; it is not used to refer to romantic or brotherly love. His love is far greater and deeper than that. It is not conditional or based upon us meeting a number of requirements. God loves the unlovable and undeserving because it is His nature to do so. Our Heavenly Father's love is the foundation of everything He does.

GOD IS LOVE

Reading through the Bible we learn that humanity was alienated from God due to our sin. We rejected Him and He gave us over to ourselves. We also learn that we have all sinned and fallen short of God's glory (see Romans 3:23). Romans 3:10 points out that none of us is righteous. In our natural state,

INSPIRATION 4: INHALE LOVE

none of us seeks God, none of us does good, and we have all turned away from God. (see Romans 3:12)

The state of mankind since the Fall is one of rebellion and disobedience. Jeremiah 17:9 reveals man's inner condition: "The heart is deceitful above all things and beyond cure. Who can understand it?"

Our innermost beings are so corrupted by sin that even we don't understand it. We have yet to fully appreciate the extent to which our sin has tainted us. Yet, despite our disobedience and inability to perfectly keep God's law, He decided to make the Perfect Sacrifice to save us from ourselves.

God spared us His wrath and instead poured out His love. He did not wait for us to start following His law perfectly as a condition for atoning for our sin. Instead, God devised a plan in which He would become a man and live amongst His people (John 1:14). He experienced our humanity in the flesh and then offered Himself willingly to stand in our place as atonement for our sin.

God did not do this because we are lovable. He did it because He is love. God can't do anything but love, because love is the essence of who God is. God loves because it is His character and the expression of His being.

> *And so we know and rely on the love God has for us. God is love. Whoever lives in love lives in God, and God in him.*
> (1 JOHN 4:16)

Even if you tried, there is nothing you can do, nothing you can say, to keep God's love from you. Nothing can separate you from His love.

For I am convinced that neither death nor life, neither angels nor demons, neither the present nor the future, nor any powers, neither height nor depth, nor anything else in all creation, will be able to separate us from the love of God that is in Christ Jesus our Lord. (Romans 8:38-39)

LOVE ONE ANOTHER

In the same way that God loves us unconditionally, He commands us to love others:

> *"A new command I give you: Love one another. As I have loved you, so you must love one another."*
> (John 13:34)

But loving others unconditionally, as God does, does not come easily. Because of our fallen nature, loving others in spite of how they treat us does not come naturally to us. Apart from God, we are incapable of producing this type of love. If we are to love as God does, that love can only come from its true source, God.

When we became God's children, He poured out His love into our hearts. Because the Spirit of God is living in us, and because God is love, love is living in us. Through the Holy Spirit, we have been empowered to love in the way that God loves.

We must inhale God's love and fully receive it into our spirits. We must allow God's love to flow freely in and through us and

INSPIRATION 4: INHALE LOVE

back out to others. Because of God's love for us, we are now capable of loving one another. When others have an encounter with us, they should experience God's love—His love should be evident in our words and our deeds.

Love is not selfish or self-centered; instead, it is about self-sacrifice. You learn to put others' needs above your own. Many people do "good" things, but they do not do it out of love. But doing "good" things is not enough—*why* you do them is equally important.

People do good things for different reasons. Some simply do them to boast; others are looking for recognition. Some people help others so they can feel that they are better than those they are helping. There are all kinds of motivations for doing good things. Make sure that your motives are pure—everything you do must be motivated by love.

Man sees what you do outwardly, but God is looking at what's going on with you inwardly. Is love truly in your heart? Do you do what you do for others simply out of love? If you are helping others for any reason beside love, you might as well do nothing.

> *If I give all I possess to the poor and surrender my body to the flames, but have not love, I gain nothing.*
> (1 CORINTHIANS 13:3)

God knows your heart. Make sure your motives are pure and everything you do is out of love.

BOUND TOGETHER BY LOVE

In the thirteenth chapter of Paul's letter to the Corinthians, he describes what love is and what love is not. (see 1 Corinthians 13:4-7)

1. Love is patient.
2. Love is kind.
3. Love does not envy.
4. Love does not boast and is not proud.
5. Love is not rude or easily angered.
6. Love keeps no records of wrongs.
7. Love rejoices in the truth.

You can refer to these as effective strategies for how you should love others and attract more love into your life. Find new ways to love your family, coworkers, neighbors, and even strangers. Determine in your spirit to interject more love into your daily interactions with others.

Loving others as God loves you is the greatest use of your life. When you live your life with this type of love, it will never fail you. Paul points out to us the magnitude of God's love. It is important to have faith in God and have hope in His promises, but the greatest virtue we should strive to possess is love.

> *And now these three remain: faith, hope and love. But the greatest of these is love.*
> (1 CORINTHIANS 13:13)

Love—even more than hope and faith—overcomes evil. It binds and unites the universe in harmony. It unites us to God and binds all of God's creation into one kingdom. It is love that sent Jesus into this world to save us, and that same love is keeping us today.

Love is living within us and allowing us to love and care for one another. We are saved by faith and we are able to hold on through the difficulties of life because of hope. But it is love that is the foundation of God's Kingdom. Love binds the Creator and all of His creatures into one.

LOVE YOURSELF FROM THE INSIDE OUT

There are so many things that we want to change about ourselves. While we should take good care of our bodies and present ourselves in the best manner possible, going to such extremes as bleaching our skin or having cosmetic surgery to the point that we are unrecognizable is a sign of a deeper issue. It shows that we do not truly love ourselves and we believe that after we reach some point of change, we will finally be able to look into the mirror and love what we see.

But after all of the changes, we still find that we are empty and hollow on the inside—because love starts from within, not without. Love yourself from the core of your being—from the inside out. Your body is just a shell that will one day fade away. *It is your spirit that you must be concerned with making as beautiful as possible*, so concentrate on developing your character and becoming beautiful from the inside out.

Learn how to shower yourself with love. If you are a single woman, it is even more important, because you won't have a man to pour out his love on you. You need to know how to love on yourself. Speak loving words to yourself; refuse to speak words of hatred into your spirit. Put away self-hatred talk like, "I hate my lips," "I hate my hair," and "I hate my hips." You may think nothing of it, but these words are hurting instead of helping you.

The power of life and death is in the tongue. (See Proverbs 18:21) When you speak such words of hatred to yourself, you are suffocating your spirit of the unconditional love it deserves. Over time, you may become depressed or develop low self-esteem without realizing where it originated. Cast down such negative thoughts when they enter your mind. Speak love to every part of your body, even if it is a part that you would like to change.

When you fail to love yourself adequately, you may find that you allow others to disrespect and mistreat you. You may seek love in the wrong places. Many people buy things to fill the void and emptiness inside them; some turn to drugs or alcohol or unhealthy relationships. Many try to fill the void with material things and spend money they don't have to fill that void; still others try to fill their emptiness with food.

Nothing will replace the void you feel except the uncompromising love of God. When you truly get it down in your spirit that God loves you and fully come to love yourself, you will realize that all the love you need is already within you. You won't go looking for it in anyone or anywhere else.

Once you fully embrace God's love and inhale it into your spirit, you will be in the position to breathe love into the life of others. Open up and allow God's love to flow freely into your spirit. Exhale and release all hatred towards yourself and

INSPIRATION 4: INHALE LOVE

others. Let go of any toxic thoughts of you being unworthy and undeserving of God's abounding love. God's love for you is unlimited and unconditional. God loves you not because of who you are, but because of Who He is—He is Love. As you release the toxic thoughts that keep you from loving yourself and others fully, you will create space to receive more of God's love. You are closer to it than you may think. Just breathe—living a life full of love is just a breath away.

INSPIRATION 5:
Inhale Hope

Holding On, Patiently Expecting

> *May the God of hope fill you with all joy and peace as you trust in Him, so that you may overflow with hope by the power of the Holy Spirit.*
> (ROMANS 15:13)

In the previous chapter, we worked on inhaling and receiving God's love. In this chapter, we will begin to flow and grow with God's inspired Word on **hope**.

"Hope" is one of those words that often gets misused, like "love." It is something that we often use in casual conversations. We say things like "I hope it doesn't rain today," "I hope you feel better," and "I hope I get the job promotion." When it is used this way, it is often no more than wishful thinking.

The type of hope I want you to inhale and get down in your spirit is far more powerful than that. It is a spirit of hope that can only be found in God. When I think of this type of hope, my spirit begins to leap. Hope is very dear to me because my middle name is "Hope." I define hope as holding on, patiently expecting.

What are you to hold on to? Hold on to God's unchanging hands. Hold on to the promises of God. Hold on to the vision He has given you for your life. Hold on to the hopes and dreams He has placed in your heart. I'm convinced that many of us let go too easily. We are quick to abandon our goals and dreams when things do not turn out perfectly on our first attempt.

TURN YOUR LEMONS OVER TO GOD

And we know that all things work together for good to them that love God, to them who are the called according to his purpose.
(Romans 8:28 KJV)

This verse does not say that all things will be good. It says that all things will work *together* for good. One of the key ingredients in an ice-cold glass of sweet lemonade is the lemon. The lemon is sour, bitter, and hard to taste if you suck on it alone. But if you squeeze it into a glass of water and mix in the right amount of sugar, you end up with a very flavorful, sweet treat.

When you isolate different incidents that occur in your life and choose to focus on them alone, it is easy to become bitter and discontented. Taken in isolation, your situation seems far from good. That experience may have caused you great hurt and pain; you don't understand it and you cannot make sense of it. You don't comprehend it, but God sees the big picture. He knows that in the end, it will all work out to your advantage. He uses every circumstance in your life to get you to where He wants you to be.

Don't get stuck on that one issue. Refuse to sit around and suck on the bitter lemons that life has handed you. Instead, take those lemons and turn them over to God. Allow Him to squeeze them into His holy glass of water and add the sweetness of Jesus. When you mix it all together, you end up with something of great taste and flavor—so instead of sucking on lemons, God wants you to sip on lemonade.

We don't like the "bad" things that we face in our lives, but God allows them because they help to develop character in us. They help us to grow, become humble, and get stronger. What is lemonade without the lemon? It's just sweet water. It is the bitter lemon that gives the lemonade its flavor. You may not appreciate the pain that you are going through now, but God is going to use it to flavor your life! It will take time to turn things around. It may turn around in a few days or it may take months or even years, but it *will* turn around. In the meantime, you need to muster up the strength to hold on.

MY MIDDLE NAME IS HOPE

I understand all too well that holding on is easier said than done. From 2003 to 2004, in less than two years, I experienced three major life-altering events. I went through a painful divorce, leaving me as a single mom to raise my three-year old son alone. I lost my job during a major industry downturn and the sum total of my retirement savings. But worse of all, I lost my dear sister, Andrea, to a disease that caused her body to turn on itself.

It seemed as if all hell was breaking lose in my life, all at one time. The enemy tempted me to lose all hope, but I refused. I spoke to him and said, "You must not know who I am. My middle name is Hope!" The very name that kids used to tease me about when I was a child, God was using to show me that all was not lost.

INSPIRATION 5: INHALE HOPE

When the burdens, pressures, and stressors of life are weighing you down, it's hard to keep holding on. In life, you may have faced many hurts and disappointments. It can be easy to become bitter and sour and lose all hope of things ever getting better. Things may seem bleak and dark in your life right now, as if nothing is going right—as soon as you manage to take one step forward, you seem to get knocked back two.

You may be having difficulties in your finances. Maybe your health or that of someone you love is at a less-than-optimum level. Your children may not be shaping out to be what you imagined. You may be having problems in your marriage. Or maybe you are single and losing hope of ever finding the right mate for you.

The obstacles you face seem to be getting more difficult and occurring more frequently. You have tried to remain optimistic, but it seems like the more you try to do right, the more that seems to go wrong. You understand that God may be trying you, but you are beginning to grow weary under the repeated tests. It seems unfair for one person to have to endure so much.

"What did I do to deserve such misery?" you may ask. "Why are You allowing these things to keep happening to me, God?" Facing setback after setback, you begin to lose your zest for life. You slowly begin to accept that this is just your lot in life and that things are not going to get much better, so you might as well quit hoping.

EXPECT THE UNEXPECTED

You may have been disappointed so many times that you have come to expect things to not go in your favor. Over time, you have developed a negative disposition towards your life. You have learned to simply not get your hopes up so you won't be disappointed. Your attitude is, "If I don't expect much, then I won't be disappointed when my desires don't come to pass."

Getting your hopes up high and dreaming big feels like it comes with too much risk—if things do not turn out as you hoped, it's too painful and depressing. It seems much safer to minimize your risks by being *realistic* and maintaining low expectations. Then, if things do not work out in your favor, you won't be so disappointed.

This may be a safer way to play it in life, but playing it safe never led anyone to do great things. If you want great rewards, you must be willing to take great risks. In trying to guarantee that you will never get hurt again, you may also be guaranteeing that you will never see your dreams come to pass.

Your financial advisor would advise you to determine your risk tolerance level. If you have a high tolerance for risk, you might be advised to invest in the stock market where the potential for gains is high. If your risk tolerance is very low, you may be advised to invest in the bond market where the risk for loss is greatly minimized. But the low potential of loss also means a low potential for great gains. Decide the level of risk you are willing to take. God promises that He is a safe bet.

If you believe something will not happen, it probably won't—it becomes a self-fulfilling prophecy. Your words and actions usually fall in line with your thoughts. If you think you will never be able to launch your dream business and make it successful, your words will probably follow suit and it will be unlikely that

INSPIRATION 5: INHALE HOPE

it will succeed. You will speak those words of negativity into your spirit and to others.

The power of life and death is in the tongue (Proverbs 18:21), and you may be killing your dreams with your own tongue. Because you think it will not happen and you repeatedly tell yourself it won't, your actions will fall in line with that disbelief. It is unlikely that you will take the necessary action steps to daily work towards your dream of launching your business.

Why would you waste your time, when you've already convinced yourself that it's not going to be successful in the first place? At the end of the day, your business is not successful, not because it *could* not be successful, but because you did not *expect* it to be successful. We normally get what we expect.

It is time to reevaluate your expectations in life. What are you anticipating from God? What are you hoping for? You need to start expecting more from God. You serve a great God who is anxious to bless you in a great way.

> *"For I know the plans I have for you," declares the LORD, "plans to prosper you and not to harm you, plans to give you hope and a future."*
> (JEREMIAH 29:11)

God has great plans for you. He intends to bless you and promote you beyond your wildest imaginations. Expect God to do what He said. If He has given you a great vision for your life, expect it to come to pass. If He has put a desire in your heart, expect Him to manifest it in your life. You have to raise your expectations.

HOLDING ON, PATIENTLY EXPECTING

Stop looking down and getting depressed over your situation and start looking up to your God. Expect God to show up and do a new thing in your life. Expect God to heal your body. Expect Him to bring you out of debt. Expect Him to bring the right opportunities into your life at the right time. Expect Him to restore your relationships.

God has not forgotten you. You may currently be in a season of your life where times are hard. Things may not be working out as you had hoped for. You may feel that your prayers are falling on deaf ears. But each morning that you wake up, learn to embrace the day with a fresh new attitude. Expect this day to be the day that God is going to turn things around in your favor. God's mercies are new every day. Each day presents you with fresh new hope.

> *It is of the LORD'S mercies that we are not consumed, because His compassions fail not. They are new every morning: great is thy faithfulness. The LORD is my portion, saith my soul; therefore will I hope in Him.*
> (LAMENTATIONS 3:22-24 KJV)

God promises that those who put their hope in Him will not be disappointed (see Isaiah 49:23). Notice that your hope must be in God, our Heavenly Father, and *not* on earthly things. When you put your hope in Him, you will not be disappointed. Not everything you desire will come to pass when you want it or how you want it—but God promises that if you keep your hope in Him, in the end, everything will work out for your good. We have a limited perspective, but God sees the big picture. He knows the great plans that He has for you. He knows why He allows you to go through certain trials and tribulations. He knows that in the end, you will come out of it

INSPIRATION 5: INHALE HOPE

better than you went into it. Your job is simply to trust God and keep your hope alive in Him.

When Ms. Hopelessness and Ms. Despair show up to steal your hope, hold on to it and refuse to give it up. When you are tempted to have low expectations and not anticipate God's best, shake off that negativity.

Allow God to breathe a fresh new breath of hope into you today. Allow Him to resurrect your dreams and breathe new hope into your spirit. Exhale and release every negative thought and emotion that tries to bind you in a state of hopelessness.

Refuse to give up on the promises of God. Take a deep breath and draw in new hope for your marriage, your finances, your health, and your children. An exciting new life infused with hope and great anticipation is closer than you think. Just Breathe. Your new life of hope is just a breath away.

INSPIRATION 6:
Inhale Faith

Stepping Out On the Promises of God

Now faith is the substance of things hoped for, the evidence of things not seen.
(Hebrews 11:1 KJV)

In the previous chapter, we were inspired with hope. In this chapter, we will begin to flow and grow with God's inspired Word on **faith**.

Hope and faith are very similar and work in tandem, but there is a distinction between the two. Hope is a dream of something that is either wanted or needed, but faith is what turns that dream into a substance or reality.

Without "things hoped for," there would be no need for faith. And without faith, hope is nothing more than wishful thinking. Hope is a good and positive expectation of the future. But faith goes beyond that and says, not only do I expect it to happen, I believe that it is already done.

Many people have hope and are anxiously awaiting results, but they lack the settled confidence and present assurance that faith offers. Faith is a spiritual substance. When you have this

INSPIRATION 6: INHALE FAITH

spiritual substance in you, it communicates to you a certain inner knowing that the thing you are hoping for is already done, even before you see any material evidence of it. You believe that it has already been established in the spiritual realm; you are just waiting for it to manifest itself in the physical realm.

To have faith is to believe in something or someone, to fully trust, to be so confident that you base your actions on what you believe. You are so convinced of the truthfulness of that in which you believe that it moves you to act accordingly. Faith in God, then, is having the kind of trust and confidence in Christ that leads you to commit your whole soul to Him as your Savior. Faith in God must be from the heart. It is not merely intellectual; it is spiritual.

For it is with your heart that you believe and are justified, and it is with your mouth that you confess and are saved.
(ROMANS 10:10).

We are to believe in God with our hearts and not our minds. God goes beyond our human understanding and comprehension. We cannot put Him in a test tube, measure His greatness, and conduct scientific experiments on Him. Our brains do not have the capacity to comprehend the power of God. With a humbled heart, we fully accept the great sacrifice that Christ made for us and fully believe in the finished work of Jesus on the cross. We have blessed assurance that not only did Jesus die for our sins, but on the third day, He was raised from the dead. He got up with all power in His hands—all power over both life and death. When we confess this belief from our heart and with our mouth, we are saved by grace.

FAITH MOVES MOUNTAINS

Jesus said in Mark 11:23, "I tell you the truth, if anyone says to this mountain, 'Go, throw yourself into the sea,' and does not doubt in his heart but believes that what he says will happen, it will be done for him." You have the power within you to remove mountains of obstacles in your life. Learn how to speak to your mountains and command them to move. Instead of speaking words of doubt, that things will never change, speak words of faith so that this, too, shall pass.

It's not enough to just speak it, though—you must truly believe it in your heart. When you truly have faith in God, you will be able to call things that are not yet in existence as though they were already in existence (see Romans 4:17).

Even though what you are waiting on has not shown up yet and is not in existence, you are to claim it as if it is already done. Your ability to do so is founded in your full confidence that God has the ability to create something out of nothing. He has full power to make a way out of no way.

It's time to start calling some things into existence in your life. Your healing is coming—*call it*. You are getting out of debt—*call it*. God will open up the right doors and shut the wrong ones—*call it*. Your child will turn around—*call it*. You will become all God created you to be and do all that He created you to do—*call it*!

You have to learn to start speaking things into your life. The power of life and death is in your tongue. (See Proverbs 18:21) With your mouth alone, you can kill your dreams or you can

INSPIRATION 6: INHALE FAITH

give new life to them. Use your faith-filled words to rekindle your spirit and restore your hope in the promises of God.

> He replied, "If you have faith as small as a mustard seed, you can say to this mulberry tree, 'Be uprooted and planted in the sea,' and it will obey you."
> (LUKE 17:6)

You may feel like you have not grown to be this great woman of faith yet. But the good news is that God can work with even a small amount of faith. A mustard seed is a very tiny seed, but God used that as an example to demonstrate that He can do great things with faith as small as this little seed.

How can faith the size of a mustard seed move problems the size of a mountain? How can itsy, bitsy, small, tiny, little faith, move big problems and obstacles that seem so insurmountable and immovable? It's not your tiny faith moving the mountain—it's your great God in whom you put your faith.

PRAY IN FAITH

> And without faith it is impossible to please God, because anyone who comes to Him must believe that He exists and that He rewards those who earnestly seek him.
> (HEBREWS 11:6)

If you desire to please God, you must believe in Him and have full confidence in His Word. You must know in your spirit that His promises are real and that His Word cannot return void. Know that God is a rewarder of those who diligently seek Him. You cannot enter into His presence if you doubt His existence. If you did not believe that God would hear and answer your prayers, there would be no motivation to call upon Him. It is impossible to make an acceptable approach unto God without this belief. We enter into the presence of God and approach His throne of mercy and grace through Christ and by our faith.

> *Therefore I tell you, whatever you ask for in prayer, believe that you have received it, and it will be yours.*
> (MARK 11:24)

God requires that you pray in faith. It does you no good to ask Him for something if you do not believe He has the power to deliver. Believe that not only does He have the *ability* to give you what you are asking for, but that He also has the *desire* to give it to you. It's one thing to know that God can bless you; it's another to know that He *wants* to bless you.

God has great plans for you. He plans to prosper and promote you beyond your imagination. God is able to bless you above and beyond what you can possibly ask or think (see Ephesians 3:20). Rely upon the power of the Holy Spirit abiding within you to teach you how to pray in faith.

We often go to God with prayers that demonstrate low expectations. We pray and ask God to just help us get by; just help us survive: "God, if you'll just help me find a job to pay my bills, I'll be happy." "God, if you'll just help me keep a roof over my head, I'll be grateful."

The Scripture says that we have not because we ask not (see James 4:2). We go to God with such small requests and then we wonder why we come away with so few blessings. Do not insult God with your low expectations. You may believe that going to God with small requests shows that you are humble, but God wants you to understand that He can accomplish great things.

IT'S ON THE WAY

The moment you put in your request to God, believe that it is on the way. When I walk into a store and purchase something, I am able to take it home with me right away. But when I shop online, I have to deal with delayed gratification, because I have to wait for the items to arrive. It requires patience, but at least I get an immediate confirmation—a promise that the goods are on the way.

Your faith is like the confirmation slip in your heart that your goods are on the way. You sense it in your heart. The actual manifestation will come later, but you have a settled confidence that it's already done. You know that it has already been accomplished in the spiritual realm—you are just waiting for it to manifest itself in the physical realm. Until then, you will firmly hold on to your confirmation that it's on the way.

Your blessings are on their way. Your deliverance is on the way. Your healing is on the way. Your new job is on the way. The restoration of your finances is on the way. Believe that, if it is in God's will, what you requested will show up in due time. It may not show up on *your* time table, but it *will* show up—in God's perfect timing.

> *For we walk by faith, not by sight.*
> (2 Corinthians 5:7 KJV)

I'll believe it when I see it is a popular phrase, but faith is all about believing it *before* you see it. Think about it. You don't need faith to believe something that you already see. As Christians, we believe in God, even though we do not see Him. We believe in Heaven and that Jesus has gone to prepare a great place for us. We have faith in the invisible and intangible promises of God.

We cannot see and touch many things that the Word promises us, but we have full confidence that those things are real. We put our full faith in God's Word and accept it as absolute truth. It is all the proof and evidence that we need to be fully convinced that Jesus will return for us and take us into Eternity to live with Him forever in Paradise. The faith that we rely upon to believe that God is real is the same faith that we must draw upon to pull us through these challenging times.

PRAY IN HIS WILL

You may be asking, "But what if it never shows up?" "What if I pray and believe but I still don't get what I want?" This is a very valid question and many even turn away from God because they feel that God is not real since they believed but did not receive what they were seeking. I want to be very clear here. We have to balance our faith in God with His will for our lives. God requires that we have faith when we approach Him with our requests. But He does not promise that we are going to get everything that we ask for. God is not going to operate outside of His will. He knows the perfect plans He has for you. When we approach the Throne of Grace, we are to ask and believe that His will, not ours, be done. Your faith says, "I trust and believe God's will to be carried out in my life." If it is God's will for me to get the new job, then I trust Him to give me the job. If it is God's will for me to get married, then I know He will send the right person into my life at the right time. If it is God's will for me to be healed, then I believe that He will heal my body in due time.

INSPIRATION 6: INHALE FAITH

When you don't understand the principle of God's will, it becomes easy to become bitter and turn your back on God when things don't go your way. My family is firmly founded in our faith in Christ. We, along with our church family and a host of others sent up many prayers for my sister Andrea to be healed and delivered from her illness. But instead of being restored to full health, God took her home to be with Him. Does this mean that prayer does not work? Does it indicate that all of us had a lack of faith and no one had a strong enough belief to intercede on her behalf? Does this conclude that God is not on the Throne and all of this faith "stuff" is not real? This is exactly what some will lead you to believe.

Many leave the faith and fall away from God because they fail to understand that God's will shall always prevail. It doesn't matter how badly we want something, if it is not in God's will, it will not be done. We don't understand why God allows certain things to happen or not happen. The mysteries of this world belong to God. Our job is to trust Our Father and believe that He knows best. We are to put our hope and faith in Him and know that He has our best interests at heart.

Even when we experience trauma and pain and things seem to be totally out of whack, we know that God is in complete control. We pray for what we need and desire, but when God gives us the answer, we accept and trust that we are His children and that our Father knows what's best for us.

When my sister died there was no longer any need to pray for her to be healed. My prayer then shifted to asking God to give me and my family the strength to accept the things we could not change. I prayed that God would use that situation to make me better and not bitter. He answered that prayer and I know that I am a stronger and better woman today because of it.

We simply have to remember that God is not our puppet and we cannot pull His strings. Having faith in God is not simply about naming it and claiming it. Yes. Name it and claim it and believe it. But...don't become bitter if you don't receive it. Trust that God knows best and always pray that His will be done.

TUNE IN TO THE GOOD NEWS

Consequently, faith comes from hearing the message, and the message is heard through the word of Christ.
(Romans 10:17).

Some people watch the news in the evening, listen to the radio news in the morning on the way to work, and then listen to bad news from coworkers all day. If this is your only source of information, it is easy to see how you could develop a negative outlook on life. Hearing negative news reports on a daily basis can easily lead to living a life based on fear.

This is why it is so important for you to tune in to God's Word as often as you can. You need a way to counter the negative messages that you are receiving from other sources. In Romans, we learn that faith comes from hearing God's Word. If you want to increase your faith, you need to put yourself in the position to hear God's Word as often as you can. If you hear something over and over, you will begin to believe it. Make sure that you are tuning in to God's Good News more than you are hearing negative news from reporters who rely on bad news to keep their ratings up.

PUT YOUR TRUST IN GOD

God took the children of Israel through the desert on their way to the Promised Land. He needed to develop their character to prepare them for the land of promise that was awaiting them. One of the primary character traits He wanted to develop in them was their faith. God wanted them to learn to trust and depend upon Him for their every need. He provided manna for them every day. They were not allowed to store it up; they had to learn to trust Him to provide fresh, new manna each day.

You may feel that you are in a desert season of your life right now, but you need to know that God still provides, even in the desert. You may not have a stock of reserves to turn to, but you have your God and He owns everything! Like many others, you may have lost a lot during this recession. But sometimes we have to lose everything before we realize that God *is* our everything. God is our all in all. Whatever you need, you can find it in God. God wants you to learn to trust and depend on Him for your every need.

When we have so much, we can begin to believe that we do not need God. When we have a steady paycheck coming in, a surplus of money, plush retirement savings, and houses that are greatly appreciated, we may begin to believe that we are in control. We may start to think more highly of ourselves than we ought to. We may start to put our confidence in ourselves instead of our God.

So, sometimes God has to humble us. He has to allow us to get to a place so low that we can't do anything but look up to Him to find the way out. When we find ourselves in situations that we cannot get ourselves out of and we have no one else to turn to, we can't do anything but turn to God. It is in these times that we remember Who made us and Who keeps us. It is during these times that we rediscover our faith in a fresh, new way.

While others are losing all hope and faith, this is the time to rebuild your faith and trust God on a higher level. You can be the testimony that others need to hear. Others will be moved by your great faith and want to know your God for their own deliverance.

I pray that during these challenging times, you flow and grow in faith. It is time to tell Ms. Doubt and Ms. Fear to take a hike. They have long overstayed their welcome. You are ready to inhale faith and welcome it into your spirit. Your thoughts, words and actions will no longer be dominated by fear. You have no doubt that God will prosper you.

You know that your best days are ahead of you and not behind you. You will walk, talk, think, and act as if you are already blessed because you know that you are. Release any negative thoughts of fear that threaten to hold you back and walk forward in the new faith-filled life that you are committed to living. Your new fulfilling life of faith is closer than you think. Just Breathe. Your faith-filled life is just a breath away.

INSPIRATION 7:
Inhale Patience

Waiting and Trusting that God is in Control

But they that wait upon the LORD shall renew their strength; they shall mount up with wings as eagles; they shall run, and not be weary; and they shall walk, and not faint.
(Isaiah 40:31 KJV)

In the previous chapters, we inhaled hope and faith. In this chapter, we will begin to flow and grow with God's inspired Word on **patience**.

I defined hope as holding on, patiently expecting, and faith as the substance of things hoped for. Both hope and faith require that we have patience. Patience is one of the most valuable virtues in the Christian life—it is a fruit of the Spirit. As Christians, we must learn to wait on the things we are hoping for and believing God will provide. God's Word is full of hope and promises, and we put our full confidence in Him and trust that He will do just what He said. But we must patiently wait for God to deliver on those goods that He has promised us.

When I order products online, I am told the date on which I can expect to have those items arrive. I have to wait on them, but I have a date to look forward to. When a woman is pregnant, she

INSPIRATION 7: INHALE PATIENCE

has a due date. She has a date around which she can expect the baby to arrive. You may be pregnant with promise right now and you are expecting your baby to arrive at any time, but you don't know exactly when.

The promises of God do not come with a delivery date. We do not know if what we are waiting for will be coming tomorrow, next month, next year, or ten years from now. It is hard to hold on and keep expecting when you do not know how long you are going to have to hold on to that expectation, but this is why hope is about *holding on, patiently expecting.*

Patience is a big part of it. You have hope and faith and you expect and believe that it is going to arrive, but you don't know how and you don't know when. It requires great patience to wait on something when you have no clue about when it may arrive. Waiting is probably one of the most difficult things we all must do as Christians.

WILL YOU WAIT?

But they that wait upon the LORD shall renew their strength; they shall mount up with wings as eagles; they shall run, and not be weary; and they shall walk, and not faint.
(Isaiah 40:31 KJV)

When we wait on God, He strengthens us and enables us to endure things that we could not bear on our own. In our natural state, without God, we would probably break under the weight of it all. But with the power of God, we are able to remain steadfast and keep holding on. In God we are renewed, reenergized, and made ready to face whatever life has to offer.

Waiting on the Lord enables us to walk out our faith in our daily lives. We are able to keep pressing on and not grow weary because the patience of God is in us. We do not faint at the first sign of trouble, but we patiently hold on to the promises of God because we know that they will come forth in our lives in due time.

THE PATIENCE OF JOB

As Christians, we strive to have the patience of Job. Job was a righteous man, yet God allowed Satan to afflict great pain upon him. He lost his children, his wealth, and his health. His friends turned their backs on him and his wife told him to curse God and die. (see Job 2:9)

Yet, in spite of his great trials and tribulations, Job refused to curse God with his lips. At one point, he did question God and wanted an explanation of why God would allow him to endure such suffering, but in the end, he realized that God was fully in control. God was still on the throne and had not forsaken him. Job determined to continue to trust in the Lord and wait on Him for deliverance.

> *Though he slay me, yet will I trust in him: but I will maintain mine own ways before him.*
> (JOB 13:15 KJV)

Job was saying that even though God allowed those afflictions to come upon Him, he would still continue to trust in God. All of his comforts had been removed and replaced with agony and pain. Yet, he still maintained his faith in God. Job did not fall into self-pity and blame God for allowing him to fall into

INSPIRATION 7: INHALE PATIENCE

the hands of Satan. He did not understand it because he was a righteous man, but he trusted that God was in control.

Because of Job's faithfulness and patience in God, everything taken from him was restored. He was blessed in the end with more than he had in the beginning. After all he had gone through, the Lord blessed and delivered him. Because Job maintained the right attitude, God blessed him and restored all that he had lost, and then some.

You may be going through a tough situation right now. You may be facing difficult circumstances. Maybe you have lost your job, your home, or your entire life savings. Your relationships may be suffering or perhaps you are facing serious complications with your health. In times of great suffering, it is easy to lose sight of God; it is easy to start questioning whether God is still on the throne.

Maybe you have been holding on for some time now, waiting for deliverance, but your patience is wearing thin. The enemy has probably convinced you that God has forsaken you. He may tempt you by whispering in your ear things like: *Why don't you just give up? God is not going to show up anyway, so just curse God and die.* You may have begun to sink into depression and despair—you don't know how much longer you can hold on.

It is during these desperate times that you must get into the Word of God and surround yourself with His hope and promises. Refuse to give up on God. Dig deep within your spirit and discover the patience of Job. It will give you the strength that you need to continue during difficult times. Develop the attitude of Job and let the enemy know that you will not give up on God. You will trust in the Lord and wait on Him to show up and turn your situation around.

God can turn things around in a second. Just one touch of God, and you will be healed. Believe that at any moment, God is going to restore your relationships, your finances, and your health. He is going to bless you with more than you had before. God will give you "double for your trouble." Put the enemy on notice.

You will not turn your back on God because you know God has not turned His back on you. You may not understand *why* God is allowing you to go through what you are going through now, but you know He *is* in control. What the enemy meant for your harm, God will use for your good. While you are waiting on God to show up, you continue to praise Him and bless His name. You refuse to curse God and die. No. Instead, you will bless the Lord and live!

THE PATIENCE OF A FARMER

> *Be patient, then, brothers, until the Lord's coming. See how the farmer waits for the land to yield its valuable crop and how patient he is for the autumn and spring rains.*
> (JAMES 5:7)

We must learn to have the patience of a farmer. When a farmer sows his seeds, he does not expect to come back the next day and find a full harvest. He cannot control the rain, the sun, or the seasons, so he must trust that everything will work out for his good. In due time, the crops will grow and his harvest will arrive. In the meantime, because he is expecting the harvest, he prepares for it.

INSPIRATION 7: INHALE PATIENCE

Your job is to sow your seeds of faith and then patiently and expectantly wait on the harvest to arrive. You cannot control things that are only in God's hands. Patiently wait for the development of His will, by which you may obtain what you desire. There is a time for everything—there is a season to sow and then there is a season to reap what has been sown. Trust that your season of great harvest is coming. Expect that it will be arriving soon and prepare yourself for it.

Developing patience is not easy to do in today's society. The highly technical world that we live in has trained us to be impatient. We have come to expect instant gratification. We are a microwave society and we expect everything fast—right now or even sooner. We want what we want when we want it. Our busy schedules, hurried lifestyles, and technological devices have made us very impatient.

We hate to wait; we despise delays and anything that takes time is not popular. We want overnight success, instant solutions to our problems, and rapid recovery from illness. We are always on the lookout for a quick fix to our problems—the fastest way to lose weight, the shortest route to obtain wealth, the quickest way to reach our goals.

Many go out and buy things they cannot afford and get into financial trouble because they did not have the patience to save up their money before making the big purchase. Many have made poor investment decisions because they did not wait for proper counsel before moving forward. Many run out and get married to the first person that comes along because they did not have the patience to wait on God to send them the right mate.

Trust me, you had better wait! Don't rush into something and then regret it later. We often blame the enemy for our problems, but if we are honest with ourselves, we are the source of many of our own problems. Impatience and rash decisions will quickly get you into trouble. Learn to be patient and wait to make rational decisions that are led by God's wisdom. Take the time to pray and think before you act. Weigh the consequences of your actions before you make a move.

THE SARAH SYNDROME

When we pray and ask God for things, we quickly become impatient with Him when He does not act according to *our* time schedule. When things are not moving at the pace we want, we may be tempted to jump in and help move the situation along—trying to work things out in our own favor instead of waiting on God. When this urge comes over you, I encourage you to pause and look at the story of Abraham and Sarah first.

In the first book of the Bible, Genesis, we see a powerful example of what *not* to do when waiting on God. Abraham and Sarah were very old in age, yet they were still waiting on God to make good on a promise to give them a son. They had received God's blessing and His promise that they would be made into a great nation with countless descendants. (See Genesis 12:1–3)

As they grew older in age and as time passed with no sign of the promise being delivered, Sarah decided to take matters into her own hands. She decided to "help" God and devised a plan for them to have a son—which they did, through Sarah's servant, Hagar (Genesis 16:1–4). So Sarah finally got a son, Ishmael, but she also got a whole lot of trouble along with him.

INSPIRATION 7: INHALE PATIENCE

Abraham and Sarah suffered great consequences for stepping out ahead of God and trying to fulfill their own promise. Their actions led to problems in their marriage, Sarah's insecurities, and a rivalry between Sarah and Hagar. But the trouble did not end there. It also resulted in generations of strife between the descendants of Ishmael and Isaac, the son Sarah and Abraham had later.

Sarah tried to help her situation, but she only ended up hurting it. God forgave Abraham and Sarah and blessed them with a son as He had promised, but they still had to suffer the consequences of their actions.

You may be tempted to help God in fulfilling your promise. Maybe you have been waiting a long time to be delivered from a situation or perhaps you are growing weary waiting for a desire of your heart to be fulfilled. It is tempting to step in and start trying to make things happen for yourself. But if God is not in it, your plans will not work—they will fall flat and you will do more harm than good; you will set yourself back even further.

If God has made you a promise, He will fulfill that promise. Trust in His timing, and patiently wait on Him. If God did not send you that man, don't marry him. If God did not offer you that position, don't accept it. If God did not open that door of opportunity for you, don't try to pry it open on your own. Stop struggling and trying to make things happen on your own. Trust God's timing and know that He is in control.

In closing this chapter, I pray that you will be patient with yourself as you grow to become more of who God created you to be.

We must learn to be patient with God and with others, but we must also learn to be patient with ourselves.

We often become impatient and frustrated with ourselves when we are not growing and progressing as quickly as we would like. But just as a fruit tree does not mature overnight, the fruits of the Spirit will not develop in you overnight. Love, joy, peace, patience and the other five fruits of the Spirit take time to develop and grow. Becoming all that God created you to be is a process that requires patience and persistence.

Allow God to continue to breathe His hope, faith, joy, and love into your spirit. God is continually breathing in your direction and filling you with all you need to become the best you can be. Be patient with yourself—God is not through with you yet. He has much more in store for you.

Take a deep breath and release impatience and anxiety from your spirit. An exciting new life defined by patience and settled confidence in God is closer than you think. Just Breathe. Your new life of patience is just a breath away.

INSPIRATION 8:
Inhale Peace

Finding Serenity in the Midst of it All

Peace I leave with you; my peace I give you. I do not give to you as the world gives. Do not let your hearts be troubled and do not be afraid.
(John 14:27)

In the previous chapter, we inhaled patience. We discovered what it truly means to trust God and wait on Him to fulfill your needs and deepest desires. In this chapter, we will begin to flow and grow with God's inspired Word on **peace**.

It is not enough to say that you are waiting on God. *How* you wait on God is just as important. If you are whining and complaining while you are waiting, you are not walking in faith. If you are worrying the entire time you are waiting, you are not showing God that your trust is in Him. One of my favorite prayers is the serenity prayer. In it, you ask God to grant you the serenity to accept the things you cannot change. This is a powerful prayer because there are so many things that you cannot change.

You cannot change your past. Whatever hurtful things have occurred in your past, accept those things and move on.

INSPIRATION 8: INHALE PEACE

Whatever mistakes you have made and problems you have brought upon yourself, accept them and move on. You may have lost your job during the economic downturn. Accept it and move on. Your spouse may have walked out on you. Accept it and move on. You probably have lost a lot of money during the country's financial crisis. Accept it and move on. Someone may have falsely accused you or treated you unfairly. Accept it and move on.

Learn to do as Paul describes in Philippians and forget those things that are behind you and press toward what is ahead (see Philippians 3:13). You can rest assured that your best days are not behind you. Better days are up ahead. God has great plans for you. He plans to prosper and promote you. Stop worrying over those things that you cannot change. Quit trying to change things that only God can change. Take your worries, concerns, and burdens and place them in His hands. Once you release it all to Him, you can finally rest in the peace of God.

LAY DOWN YOUR BURDENS

> *"Come to me, all you who are weary and burdened, and I will give you rest."*
> (MATHEW 11:28)

You may feel that you are carrying a heavy load right now. Maybe you are weighed down with guilt over mistakes you have made in the past. You may be concerned that you have not made the kind of progress that you had hoped to make by this time in your life. You may be overloaded with worries over how you are going to pay your bills, fund your kids' college education, or how you are going to fund your own retirement now.

Maybe you are experiencing major health issues and that has you greatly concerned.

God does not want you to live in continuous distress and despair. He does not want you living under constant stress and strain. Life should not be a constant struggle. God has provided a way for you to release your burdens—He beckons you to come to Him and promises to give rest to all who do. If you are weary and have reached the point where you don't know how you can go on any longer, it is time to go to God. If you are worn out from worrying and stressing over the problems in your life, why not seek rest in God's everlasting arms?

WORRY PROFITS YOU NOTHING

This is what God asks of those who worry:

> *Who of you by worrying can add a single hour to his life?*
> (Mathew 6:27 NIV)

Jesus wisely tells us in Mathew 6 that worrying is worthless—we cannot add a single hour to our lives by worrying. He goes on to tell us that if God sees fit to take care of the lilies of the field, imagine how much *more* He will take care of you and me (see Mathew 6:30). You do not have to worry about how you will be clothed or what you will eat or drink. God will take care of you.

So, if you are not to worry, what are you to do? Jesus provides the answer to that as well. You are to seek first His kingdom and His righteousness and all other things will be added unto to you (see Mathew 6:33). God's antidote to worry is simple. He

INSPIRATION 8: INHALE PEACE

wants you to replace your worry with worship. Stop worrying over your problems and start worshipping your Problem Solver.

Jesus has already made the case that worrying profits you nothing. The only thing it accomplishes is to weaken you: spiritually, emotionally, mentally, and even physically. Constant worry can raise your blood pressure, bring on migraines, cause digestive problems, and weaken your immune system, making you more susceptible to many illnesses. If you are already battling an illness, the last thing you want to do is weaken your immune system even further with added stress and worry.

Do not be anxious about anything, but in everything, by prayer and petition, with thanksgiving, present your requests to God. And the peace of God, which transcends all understanding, will guard your hearts and your minds in Christ Jesus.
(PHILIPPIANS 4:6-7)

We are all too familiar with stress and anxiety because they are a part of everyday life. Daily, we are faced with challenges that present us with the opportunity to lose our peace. Many people are anxious over the economic challenges facing our nation today. You may have been personally affected by the massive job layoffs that swept the country during the great recession.

If you have any money in the stock market, you have no doubt experienced some level of anxiety about the sharp downturns in the market over the recent years. You may be concerned about how you will fund your retirement and what tomorrow holds for you. It is easy to fall into anxiety and to be overwhelmed with worry and fear, but Jesus tells us that we should not be concerned about our future—God holds your tomorrow.

When you find yourself falling into despair, recall what Paul tells us and be anxious for nothing. Instead, take your problems to God in prayer. When you put your trust in God, He will reward you with a peace that surpasses all understanding.

Think about that. What does it mean to have peace that surpasses all understanding? In worldly terms, it means that you probably should have lost your mind by now—because of all you have gone through, it is logical that you should have cracked under the pressure by now. But by the grace of God, instead of you walking around worrying, you are walking around worshipping! Others will see you as strange. They feel bad for you and expect you to be throwing a major pity party by now, but you somehow continue to praise God and worship Him in spite of your circumstances.

Instead of pacing the floor with worry at night, you are able to release it to God and rest in His peace. This type of peace is not found in the world and it is not understood by most. It is not found at the bottom of a bottle nor in drugs nor in the comfort of a man's arms. No. This is God's peace that surpasses all understanding. This is the type of peace that the world can't give and the world can't take away.

PEACE BE STILL

To understand this type of peace a little better, let's recall the incident in which Jesus and his disciples were all together in a boat. After a long day of ministering to the crowds, Jesus told the disciples they were going over to the other side of the Sea of Galilee. They all boarded the ship as Jesus commanded and headed out on their journey. Before they knew it, a terrible storm hit and their boat was quickly filling with water. Fearful

INSPIRATION 8: INHALE PEACE

that their boat would sink, the disciples became anxious and afraid for their lives.

What was Jesus, the Prince of Peace, doing in the midst of all this? He was sleeping like a baby in the back of the boat! The disciples were beside themselves—how could Jesus be *sleeping* when their lives were about to be swallowed up by the raging storm? Did Jesus not care about them?

> *And there arose a great storm of wind, and the waves beat into the ship, so that it was now full. And he was in the hinder part of the ship, asleep on a pillow: and they awake him, and say unto him, Master, carest thou not that we perish? And he arose, and rebuked the wind, and said unto the sea, Peace, be still. And the wind ceased, and there was a great calm.*
> (Mark 4:37-39 KJV)

As you journey through life, trying to make it to the other side like the disciples were doing, you will undoubtedly run into some storms. Have you ever felt that God was asleep in the midst of your storm? All hell seems to be breaking loose in your life. You are anxious and worried and trying to do everything within your power to keep your boat afloat. You pray to God, but it seems as if Heaven is silent in your situation. You cry out in desperation and frustration to God, "Don't you care about me? Do you not even care if I perish?"

God is saying the same to you as He said to His disciples: you have little faith. After the disciples woke Jesus, He got up and spoke to the storm. He commanded the sea, "Peace, be still." The wind and sea obeyed His command and what once was a raging storm became a calm sea of serenity. But then Jesus turned to His disciples and admonished them for their lack of faith. He could not believe that after walking with Him and witnessing Him perform miracle after miracle that they still did not trust Him.

We need not fear the terrible storm that comes upon us, because the Lord is in control of all circumstances in our lives. Nothing can happen to you that God does not allow. And if God allows it, there is a *reason* for it, even if we don't understand it yet. But God promises that He will not put more on us than we can bear.

If God has allowed you to enter a storm, He has already devised a way to get you out. You must learn to speak to your storm and command it to be still. When all hell seems to be breaking loose in your life, whisper these words: "Peace. Be still."

But the truth of the matter is that the storm is not always going to go away so quickly. You can't pray away all of your problems. Sometimes you must learn to find peace even while in the midst of the storm. Even when nothing seems to be going your way and life seems darkest, you need to look within and find the peace of God.

Like Jesus, you can rest while the storm is still raging all around you because the peace of God is in you. You know that God is still on the throne and you trust Him to take care of those things that are beyond your control. When you put your full trust in the One who has all power over the storm, you will find peace that surpasses all understanding.

INSPIRATION 8: INHALE PEACE

GUARD YOUR MIND

Many of us become all worked up, anxious, and worried just from the thoughts we have. The human brain processes thousands of thoughts each day. Think about how many of those thoughts are negative and fear based. If you are continuously thinking that the worst case scenario will happen, you will quickly lose your peace and not have the spiritual, mental, and physical strength you need to fight the battle.

Those battles you fight first begin in your mind. You must fight to hold on to your peace and refuse to allow the enemy to overtake you with anxiety and fear. Meditating on God's Word is by far the greatest way to calm your mind.

> *Finally, brothers, whatever is true, whatever is noble, whatever is right, whatever is pure, whatever is lovely, whatever is admirable—if anything is excellent or praiseworthy—think about such things.*
> (PHILIPPIANS 4:8)

Learn to consciously monitor your thoughts—to take them captive and control them. Make your thoughts work *for* you instead of *against* you by putting your thoughts under the complete authority of God and allowing the Holy Spirit to guide your thinking.

Learn to be conscious (or aware) of what you are thinking about. If your thinking is negative and fear-based, replace it with positive, faith-based thoughts. Recall God's Word and play it over and over in your mind. Replace every lie of the enemy with God's Truth.

As long as your thoughts are unsettled, your spirit will be unsettled. Once you calm your mind, you will be able to calm your inner spirit. If you desire to find rest in God, turn over your thought life to Him. Stop conjuring up bad possibilities and start thinking about all that is possible when you put your total confidence in God the Almighty.

There is nothing impossible for God. It is time to exhale all negative, fear-based thoughts that the enemy sends to keep you bound by anxiety and worry. Make a declaration that, as of this day, you will stop worshipping your problems and start worshipping your God.

As the weight of worry begins to lift from you, God will fill you with a peace that surpasses all understanding. As often as you can, find a quiet place to meditate on God's Word. Pick a Scripture, read it, and then recall it over and over again in your mind. Calm your mind, body, and spirit as you breathe deeply. Your peace is closer than you think. Just Breathe. Your peace is just a breath away.

INSPIRATION 9:
Inhale Joy
Enjoying Your Everyday Life

> *This is the day the LORD has made; let us rejoice and be glad in it.*
> (PSALM 118:24)

In the previous chapter, we inhaled peace. We discovered how to find serenity in the midst of life's trials and tribulations. In this chapter, we will begin to flow and grow with God's inspired Word on **joy**.

I do not believe that you can have authentic joy without being at peace. When you lose your peace and become unsettled in your spirit, your opportunity for joy goes along with it—but when you choose to remain in peace, you lay the foundation for experiencing joy.

When you are living in joy, you choose to enjoy your everyday life regardless of your current circumstances. Notice that I said, "you choose." Living in joy does not happen naturally—it is a choice that you make and it is one that you must make each and every day.

Every single day, we are presented with opportunities to lose our joy and peace, but each day we must wake up and declare,

INSPIRATION 9: INHALE JOY

"This is the day that the LORD has made. I will rejoice and be glad in it." (See Psalm 118:24)

Put the enemy on notice that, regardless of your circumstances, you will rejoice because you are still alive. Things may not be going exactly the way you would like right now, but you know that God is still in control. He is working behind the scenes and turning your situation around. In the meantime, you declare, "I will bless the Lord at all times. His praise will continually be in my mouth." (See Psalm 34:1 KJV)

Recognizing that staying in peace and happiness is a choice you make will free you up to enjoy your everyday life. I once heard someone say that ten percent in life is what happens to you, and the other ninety percent is how you respond to it. In other words, your reaction to a situation greatly affects the impact it will have on you.

We often feel powerless because so many things happen in our lives that are beyond our control. Many of those things we would rather have not encountered. Let's face it: stuff happens to all of us that we would prefer not to deal with. But although you may *not* be able to always control what *happens* to you, you *can* control how you choose to *respond* to it. You can choose to stay in peace and hold on to your joy. You can choose to enjoy your everyday life even when things are not going your way. Even when life is hard and your circumstances are difficult, you have the choice to remain in peace, be content and continue to praise your God. You can choose to maintain a positive outlook on life, hope for the best, and keep your faith in God. It is a daily choice that you must make.

Today you can declare, "Everything may not be going my way. I may be in a season of dryness. My situation may be bleak and dark, but the Scripture says that weeping may endure for a night but joy comes in the morning." (See Psalm 30:5)

You will not always be upbeat—that is not realistic. We are human and there is a season for everything. There is a time to weep and a time to laugh, a time to mourn and a time to dance (see Ecclesiastes 3:4). But you can proclaim, "This, too, shall pass. The same God who brought me through my last valley is the same One who will bring me through this valley." No matter how bad the situation looks, God promises that He will make it work for your good in the end. You have to hold on, knowing that your deliverance is coming. In the meantime, praise God and bless His holy Name. He is worthy to be praised.

DELIGHT YOURSELF IN THE LORD

When you continually offer up praises to God, your spirit rejoices. Your inner spirit yearns to worship God and be in His presence. When you choose to take your mind off your problems and focus on God instead, you set yourself up to experience authentic joy in the Lord. As you make Jesus the center of your joy, your happiness will begin to revolve around Him.

Many people mistakenly base their happiness on what's happening at the moment, what's going on around, and to them. If everything is going their way and lining up according to their plans, then they are happy. But the moment something they perceive as "bad" happens, their happiness blows away with the wind. People like this are happy one moment and uptight the next. Their life is an emotional roller coaster.

INSPIRATION 9: INHALE JOY

No. God does not want you to live this way. He wants you to delight yourself in Him *at all times*.

> *Delight yourself in the LORD and he will*
> *give you the desires of your heart.*
> (PSALM 37:4)

You are to seek your happiness in the Lord. Delight yourself in Him and He will give you the desires of your heart. You will not find everlasting joy outside of Jesus. The happiness that the world offers is temporary, lasting but for a moment. God offers an eternal joy that the world can't give and the world can't take away. It is not based on material things or your current circumstances; it is not dependent upon what is happening at the moment. The joy that God offers is permanent and based on the finished work of His Son, Jesus. The world's joy is based on what's happening outside of you, but God's joy is based on what's happening *in* you. You have joy because you have Jesus. Joy is deep down in your soul.

CIRCUMSTANTIAL JOY

When your joy is tied to your circumstances, it can flee at any time. The circumstances of today can, and often will, change tomorrow because they are temporary—here today, gone tomorrow. If your joy is tied up in your job, you'll lose your joy if you lose your job. If your joy is tied up in your relationship and he walks out on you, your joy will walk out with him. If your joy is tied up in your home and you lose your home, you'll lose your joy as well.

So many people lost their joy during the economic downturns that have swept multiple nations over the recent years. Many had their joy tied up in their material possessions, financial status, and job positions. When they lost those possessions and positions, they lost their joy.

Many are not happy until all circumstances line up just the way they planned them. Some have a mentality that says, "I'll be happy again when I find a new love. I'll be happy again when God heals my body. I'll be happy again when I get a job to pay these bills. I'll be happy again when my child starts acting right." No. Happiness is a *choice*. Stop basing your happiness on what's happening at the moment. Choose to be happy and hold on to your joy in *every* situation. Regardless of the circumstances, choose to be content, stay in peace, and hold on to your joy.

When your happiness is dependent upon what is happening at the moment, your life is unstable. This is a miserable way to live life. But you can be happy and hold on to your joy at all times when your joy is found in Jesus. Your attitude should be, "I have joy because I have Jesus. Jesus is the center of my joy. On Sunday, I have joy because I have Jesus. On Monday, when the traffic is bad and things are hectic in the office, I still have joy because I've still got Jesus."

Jesus does not change from day to day. God is the same today as He was yesterday and He'll be the same tomorrow. Therefore, your level of joy does not have to fluctuate up and down. If your joy is truly rooted in Jesus, it can stay constant from one moment to the next. Delight yourself in the Lord. Praise God and rejoice in Him every day regardless of your circumstances.

INSPIRATION 9: INHALE JOY

ENJOY THE JOURNEY

Do you have joy in your life every single day? Or have you convinced yourself that your particular circumstances make happiness and contentment impossible for you? Are you unhappy with yourself because of your mistakes and failures? You may feel that you have not made as much progress as you had hoped by this stage of your life, but you must learn to embrace the place where you are. Stop being so hard on yourself and enjoy your life right where you are.

Life is a journey that is filled with mountaintops and valleys, sharp curves, bumpy roads, and potholes. You may have run into a dead end and taken a detour, but God will get you back on track. Don't wait until you reach your destination before you start enjoying life. Celebrate and enjoy this journey called life and make happiness a high priority.

To enjoy life, maintain a good and positive attitude. Stay hopeful and believe that everything is going to turn out all right. Practice being positive in every situation—even if it seems to be negative at the moment, expect God to somehow use it for your good in the end. You *can* learn to be content no matter your circumstances.

> *I am not saying this because I am in need, for I have learned to be content whatever the circumstances.*
> (PHILIPPIANS 4:11)

MAKE A JOYFUL NOISE

> *O come, let us sing unto the LORD: let us make a joyful noise to the rock of our salvation.*
> (PSALM 95:1 KJV)

The Psalmist here is urging us to enter into God's presence with praise and thanksgiving. You do not have to wait until you go to church on Sunday morning to praise God—and you shouldn't! You do not have to sing out loud to make a joyful noise unto God—keep a song in your heart and praise God in your spirit.

Every time you draw near to God, you are entering into His presence. When you are driving to work and stuck in traffic, God is with you. When you are at work and dealing with difficult co-workers, God is with you. When you are at home and struggling to maintain your household, God is with you. You can praise God in all these moments.

Thank Him for being with you always and giving you the strength to make it through the day. Thank Him for being your Rock of salvation. Jesus provides the solid foundation on which we stand. No matter what happens in our lives, our salvation in Him is secure and firm. In Him we find refuge and safety and therefore should praise Him at all times.

Anger, frustration, impatience, and worry all threaten to rob you of your joy. It is time to show these negative spirits the exit door. They have long overstayed their welcome. You are ready to inhale joy and receive it into your spirit. Your thoughts, words, and actions will no longer be dominated by anger and frustration because you have declared in your spirit, "This is the day that the Lord has made and I will be glad in it."

The joy of the Lord is your strength and you gladly receive it today. Exhale and release all negative emotions of anger and frustration. Let go of worry and doubt and begin to enjoy your

INSPIRATION 9: INHALE JOY

life regardless of your circumstances. Make a determination that no matter what you are facing, you will bless God's name.

Open up and fully receive God's joy into your spirit. Rely on that joy to give you the strength you need to walk out your faith every day of your life. As you become more of who God created you to be, commit to becoming a woman full of joy. Your new life of overflowing joy is closer than you think. Just Breathe. Your joy-filled life is just a breath away.

INSPIRATION 10:

Inhale Strength

Drawing in God's Divine Power

> *I can do all things through Christ which strengtheneth me.*
> (PHILIPPIANS 4:13 KJV)

In the previous chapter, we inhaled joy. In this chapter, we will begin to flow and grow with God's inspired Word on **strength**.

God's Word reveals to us that we have the power within us to do all things through Christ. That's good to know, because we've got a lot to do. We were created for a divine purpose and God has much important work for us to do.

You can do *all* things *through* Christ, but you cannot do much (or anything at all, really) *without* Him. So how do we get this power? As we learned in the previous chapter, the joy of the Lord is our strength. If you want to build up your strength, rejoice in the Lord *at all times*—rejoice in the Lord in the morning, in the noonday, and at night; rejoice when things are good and when things are bad; rejoice when you are on the mountaintop and when you are down low in the valley; rejoice when the sun is shining bright over your life and when the dark clouds are hanging low.

INSPIRATION 10: INHALE STRENGTH

Rejoice when you get the job you want and continue rejoicing if you lose the job; rejoice when that special man walks into your life and keep on rejoicing even if he walks back out; rejoice while you are healthy and keep rejoicing while you are praying and believing God for healing. Rejoice in the Lord at all times because the joy of the Lord is your strength.

When you don't find your joy in God, you'll search for happiness outside of Him, in all the wrong places. This puts you in a weakened state of mind and makes you vulnerable. When your joy and peace are in your Heavenly Father, you become stable-minded and strong.

I understand that you may not feel very strong right now. Maybe you have been facing many struggles in your life. You may be growing weary under the heavy burdens that you carry. You have been trying to fight the good fight of faith but the constant battles in your life have worn you out. You probably are feeling that you could break under the pressure at any moment and that you don't have the strength to go on.

But *you are stronger than you think*. God will give you the strength to get through the struggles you are facing now. God is your refuge and strength in times of trouble (see Psalms 46:1). If you can learn how to lean on God and receive the strength you need, you truly can do all things through Christ. God beckons all who are weary and heavy-burdened to find rest in Him (see Mathew 11:28). If you take refuge in Him, He will build you up and strengthen you for the battles you face in life.

THE BATTLE IS NOT YOURS

Many people wear themselves out because they are trying to fight their battles on their own. But the battle is not yours to fight; it belongs to the Lord. Put your trust and faith in God and allow Him to fight your battles. You can take comfort in knowing that "greater is He that is in you than He that is in the world." (see 1 John 4:4)

The God who dwells in your heart through His Spirit is greater than anything that can come up against you. So if God is for you, who can be against you? With God on your side, you don't have to worry about the opposition you face. God has empowered you to withstand all things that come against you. That power I am referring to comes from God Himself who dwells within you.

Before Jesus died, He told His disciples that it was good for them that He was going away because He would send them the Holy Spirit to be their "Comforter" (see John 16:7). While Jesus was in His earthly body, He could only be in one place at one time, but His Spirit is everywhere, in all places, at all times, available to help in all situations.

In order to receive God's help, ask for it, believing. James tells us that we don't *have* because we don't *ask* (see James 4:2). Asking for help requires that you learn to humble yourself before God and cry out to Him in your weakness—acknowledge that you can't do anything without Him. Pray that He strengthens you to do all that you were created to do. If you hold on to your pride and try to do everything in your own strength, you will fail miserably. It is only when you totally submit yourself to God that He can begin to work a miracle through you.

INSPIRATION 10: INHALE STRENGTH

DAVID AND GOLIATH

We all know the Bible story of David and Goliath. David was just a small, young boy, but he volunteered to go up against Goliath, a strong giant. Others doubted David and thought he was foolish. They tried to talk him out of it but David trusted God to empower Him to do the unthinkable and was convinced that His God would give him the victory.

Since David insisted on going out to the battlefield, King Saul gave him his personal armor to use, but the armor was too big for David. He could not wear it, so he decided to face Goliath with only a slingshot and five smooth rocks. Everyone thought that surely David would be defeated easily by the mighty giant, but they didn't know the God that David served.

David boldly stepped out onto the battlefield to face Goliath and when Goliath ran towards him, he did not back down. Instead, he reached in his shepherd's bag and pulled out a stone. He put it in his slingshot, slung it, and hit Goliath in his forehead, killing him. With one, small stone and the mighty power of God on his side, David was victorious.

You may be facing some Goliath situations in your life right now. You may feel that you are too weak for what you are facing. But if you will believe in your God as David did, the power within you will rise up and make you a conqueror. God will add His *super* to your *natural* and make you capable of doing things you could not do apart from Him. God will give you supernatural strength so others will know that His anointing is on your life. Others will know that there's no way that you could accomplish such things in your own strength—they will want to know your God.

GOD IS GREATER THAN YOUR GIANTS

David understood God's power and knew how to draw his strength from it. When you learn to draw upon God's strength, you will begin to conquer problems that, in the past, would have conquered you.

Romans 8:37 says, "we are more than conquerors." Knowing that you are more than a conqueror gives you the confidence to face whatever comes against you. David did not run from his big problem; he faced it head on. You can't always pray your problems away—at some point, you must face what you've been fleeing. Maybe you've been running from the pain of losing a loved one, still in denial and not wanting to accept it.

Maybe you have been avoiding dealing with the pain of a divorce, afraid and not knowing how to rebuild your life and take charge of your household. Perhaps you are fighting the battle of your life and feel you don't stand a chance against the sickness you are facing. Or maybe you are facing a Goliath of mounting bills and the stress of how to make ends meet is wearing you down. Regardless of the size of the giant you're facing in your life, I'm here to remind you that your God is greater. There is no problem too difficult or too big for Him to work out.

God will give you everything you need to come out of your giant situations on top. Remember, the battle is not yours; it belongs to the Lord. Let the Lord do the fighting and be certain to give Him the glory when the battle is won.

The same resurrecting power that raised Christ from the dead is the same power living in you today. When you were saved,

INSPIRATION 10: INHALE STRENGTH

you were spiritually resurrected by the power of the Holy Spirit. You are still in the world, but you began to live above the world and be less affected by it.

With each experience of His resurrecting power, you become a little more like the resurrected Christ. You have the power to overcome the obstacles you encounter in life. You have the power within you to rise up and go forth to do what God has created you to do. Many of us don't recognize the power that is available to us because we are too busy trying to do everything in our own strength. Instead of waiting on God, we take matters into our own hands and try to handle them on our own.

But they that wait upon the LORD shall renew their strength; they shall mount up with wings as eagles; they shall run, and not be weary; and they shall walk, and not faint.
(ISAIAH 40:31 KJV)

If you try to go forth in your own strength, you shall faint and surely fall. But if you wait on God, He will give you the strength of an eagle. It is a common belief that the eagle lives much longer than other birds because he is able to reinvent himself. He loses his feathers and puts forth fresh ones, thereby renewing his youth. If you wait upon God, putting your hope and faith in Him, He will renew your strength. He will give you fresh new feathers so you can spread your wings and rise above the storms in your life. But you have to wait upon the Lord if you want to be renewed, restored, and reenergized.

Don't run ahead of Him and try to make things happen in your own strength—you will just wear yourself out and accomplish nothing. Make time to sit in God's presence each day and be renewed by His Word. Spend quality time with Him and draw upon His strength. If you wait in His presence, you will find that He is more than enough to bring you through to victory. He will build you up and give you the power you need to overcome all opposition.

GOD'S POWER IS MADE PERFECT IN YOUR WEAKNESS

I believe that many women today are not receiving the strength they need because they have a hard time admitting that they need help. Many women feel that they must appear to be spiritually strong at all times—that acknowledging their weakness makes them less of a Christian. Don't allow your pride to get in the way of receiving what you need from God. God is waiting for you to stop trying to handle things on your own so He can step in and take control. But God tends not to help you until you relinquish control over to Him.

If you are full of pride and believe that you can do it all in your own power, God is a gentleman, patient—He will step back and let you try. When you are ready to submit to His will and allow Him to take charge, He gives you the help you need. God is looking for those who are willing to be empty vessels so He can work a miracle through them.

> *But he said to me, "My grace is sufficient for you, for my power is made perfect in weakness." Therefore I will boast all the more gladly about my weaknesses, so that Christ's power may rest on me.*
> (2 Corinthians 12:9)

The apostle, Paul, is acknowledging here that God's grace was more than sufficient for what he was going through. You

INSPIRATION 10: INHALE STRENGTH

may be facing some difficult times now, but God's grace is more than enough to carry you through. God's power is not imparted to those who feel that they are strong and do not see a need for His divine intervention. Paul did not boast in his own abilities. Instead, he humbled himself and acknowledged his weaknesses, knowing that God would make him strong. He took comfort in knowing that the grace of God was with him to strengthen and comfort him in the midst of his trials. He knew that the weaker he was, the more God's power would show forth through him.

When we are weak in ourselves, we are made strong by the grace of our Lord Jesus Christ. But until we acknowledge that we are weak, God won't make us strong.

Humble yourself before God. Submit yourself to Him and accept that your Heavenly Father will build you up so you can stand firm on His Holy Word.

You may be struggling with a "poor-me," victim mentality. Maybe you have bought into the lies of the enemy and been wallowing in self-pity. Now is the time for you to rise up and declare that you are more than a conqueror. You need to show Ms. Self-pity the exit door.

God made you a victor, not a victim. You can do all things through Christ who strengthens you. Maybe you have been trying to handle things on your own but have finally realized that you can't do it without God.

We all face difficulties and challenges in our lives. The only way to overcome these obstacles is through the power of God.

DRAWING IN GOD'S DIVINE POWER

It's time to let go of your ego and acknowledge that you need God's divine power. It's time to exhale and release the mentality that convinces you that you have to do it on your own.

Now is the time to draw near to God and breathe in His Holy power. Inhale God's supernatural strength and feel your spirit rise up and prepare to overcome every obstacle that stands in your way. His divine power is closer than you think. Just Breathe. Your supernatural strength is just a breath away.

INSPIRATION 11:

Inhale Freedom

Living Life with No Boundaries

So if the Son sets you free, you will be free indeed.
(JOHN 8:36)

In the previous chapter, we inhaled strength. In this chapter, we will begin to flow and grow with God's inspired Word on **freedom** and liberate our spirit from everything that holds it captive.

Freedom is arguably one of the most treasured possessions one can enjoy. It is more valuable than power, money, and all the material possessions in the world. Many wars have been fought and plenty of blood has been shed to pay for the price of freedom.

FREEDOM IN CHRIST

There is no greater freedom than the spiritual freedom we enjoy in Christ Jesus. We have the freedom to follow God, abide in His Word, and enjoy all of the rights and privileges that come with being a child of the Most High God.

We did not always enjoy this freedom, however. Before Christ came, all of humankind was a slave to sin, separated from God, and living in a world of spiritual darkness. But God had already devised a plan to rescue the people he loved. He sent His one and only Son to be their Savior.

Only Jesus, who was without sin, could deliver those who were drowning in sin. God saw fit to reach down and pull us up out of the mess that we had made for ourselves. If you know Jesus as your Lord and Savior, you know Him as your Redeemer. He has paid the ultimate price to deliver you from the grips of sin. You are no longer a slave to sin. You are now a member of God's family.

You are His daughter and heir to His great riches. Jesus has set you free and who the Son sets free is free indeed (see John 8:36). You are free to live a full life of love, joy, peace, and harmony. God has freed you from the controlling toxic spirits of anger, envy, hatred, fear, and doubt. God saved and set you free so you can move forward in your purpose and become all He created you to be. He gave you wings to fly like an eagle and rise above the situations in life that threaten to hold you back. It's time to break free and become all you were meant to be.

Although this great freedom is available to us in Christ, too many Christians are not experiencing this freedom. There are many reasons that you may not be enjoying God's freedom and we will examine a few of them here.

THE REAL ENEMY

> *For our struggle is not against flesh and blood, but against the rulers, against the authorities, against the powers of this dark world and against the spiritual forces of evil in the heavenly realms.*
> (EPHESIANS 6:12)

In case you are not convinced, the Bible makes it clear that we are still in a war. As long as we live in this fallen world, in our earthly vessels, we will face opposition. Satan is the prince of all darkness and evil. He has an army of fallen spirits who serve him in wreaking havoc upon earth. If you are trying to do any good for God, you are guaranteed that the enemy will try to do anything to stop you. He wants your thoughts, your mind, your heart, and your soul.

Satan sets you up to wrestle with spiritual strongholds, so it is something that you find yourself struggling to break free from. It may be a negative thinking pattern, wrong mindset, toxic emotion, or self-sabotaging habit. But a stronghold is just that: it has a strong hold on you. You may try to let *it* go, but it refuses to let *you* go.

Your stronghold prevents you from moving forward and making real progress towards your promised land. It is as though you have invisible chains around your feet. Every time you try to move ahead, it seems like you are snapped back into place. Your strongholds are those spiritual areas where you seem to struggle the most. No matter how hard you try, you seem to make little progress, and become frustrated with your spiritual lack of maturity in those areas.

The good news is that God has given you the strength to loose yourself from your strongholds. You no longer have to stay bound up by your negative emotions, short temper, irrational fears, anger, hatred, and other spiritual strongholds that keep you from moving forward in your life. God has given you a full arsenal of weapons to win this spiritual warfare. But the first step to winning any war is to know your enemy inside and out.

INSPIRATION 11: INHALE FREEDOM

I believe that many of us are losing our daily battles in life because we don't even know who we are really fighting. You are not fighting your boss who refuses to promote you no matter how well you perform. You are not fighting the co-worker who chooses to stab you in the back every opportunity she gets. You are not fighting your so-called friend who betrayed you. You are not fighting your children who sometimes disobey you and you are not fighting your spouse who sometimes disappoints you.

No. The Bible makes it clear that your enemy is much more powerful than the ones before you. You are fighting evil spirits that the enemy sends to attack you. In other words, you are in a spiritual battle with an enemy you cannot see. He is invisible, but you see the real effects of the destruction he causes in your life. He is intangible and you can't touch him, but you can surely feel the devastating pain as a result of his attacks. He is an elusive enemy, but very real just the same.

So how do you fight an enemy whom you cannot touch or see? I'm sure you've heard the saying, "Keep your friends close and your enemies closer." It's much better to keep your enemies close in front of you instead of behind you. You don't want them to sneak up on you and catch you off-guard. It's hard to fight an enemy you can't see.

You can call this type of enemy a coward because he will not come forward. That is true, but, regardless of what you call him, he can do incredible damage if you do not adapt to his tactics. Satan attacks us by sending his negative spirits to take hold of our thoughts and take charge of our minds.

You must put on the full armor of God to protect your mind and guard your thoughts from the enemy. You need to aggressively protect yourself from the continuous attacks of the enemy and be on the defensive, but you must also be on the offensive—proactive. God has given us all we need to be victorious in this spiritual warfare.

DRESS FOR BATTLE

> *Therefore put on the full armor of God, so that when the day of evil comes, you may be able to stand your ground, and after you have done everything, to stand.*
> (Ephesians 6:13)

In order to keep standing under the attacks of the enemy, you must put on the full armor of God. It's interesting to note that the first piece of armor listed is truth (see Ephesians 6:14). The Gospel of Jesus Christ is the truth of God. If you stand any chance against the enemy, you must know God's Word and abide in His truth.

When you know God's truth, you can enter into spiritual warfare with a distinct advantage. It is by this truth that we come to know who our enemies really are and how they come to attack us. It is by the truth that we discover where our strength lies and how to activate the power of God within us. The enemy knows that you cannot destroy him without the truth, and that is why he does everything to convince you of his lies. But you must grab hold of the truth because the truth will set you free. Let's examine some of those truths right now.

> *Then you will know the truth, and the truth will set you free.*
> (John 8:32)

INSPIRATION 11: INHALE FREEDOM

*Jesus answered, "I am the way and the truth and the life.
No one comes to the Father except through me."*
(JOHN 14:6)

*The Word became flesh and made his dwelling among
us. We have seen his glory, the glory of the One and Only,
who came from the Father, full of grace and truth.*
(JOHN 1:14)

From these Scriptures, we can conclude that Jesus is the Truth, the Way, and the Life. Jesus is also the Word made flesh. So if Jesus is the Truth and Jesus is the Word, then the Word is the Truth. You need to know the Word because the Word is the Truth and the Truth shall set you free!

When you know the truth, you will be liberated from the lies of the enemy. When the enemy tries to convince you that you will never smile again and that you will always feel the pain you are currently feeling, you can confront him with the truth that weeping may endure for the night, but joy comes in the morning. (see Psalms 30:5)

When the enemy tries to fill your mind with thoughts that you are weak and can't make it through your current struggles, armed with the truth, you can declare that the Bible says you are more than a conqueror (see Romans 8:37). When the enemy tries to keep you bound to your past mistakes, remind him that you are now living under the grace of God (see Romans 6:14).

God has forgiven you and released you from your past. When the enemy persists that you have messed up too badly this time and God can't use you in His Kingdom, declare what Romans 8:39 says, "Neither height nor depth, nor anything else in all creation, will be able to separate us [me] from the love of God that is in Christ Jesus our [my] Lord."

WOMAN, THOU ART LOOSED!

But what happens when you have been wrestling with the same issue for so long that you don't feel like you can go on any longer? You have tried to put on the full armor of God and tried to fight the good fight of faith, but you seem to keep losing this battle. You now find yourself physically, emotionally, and spiritually weak. You have given all of the fight that was in you and now you are drained and near the end of your rope. What do you do now? You take your issue to God like we see in the story of the infirmed woman in the Bible.

The infirmed woman had an issue of blood. She had been tied to that sickness for twelve years. Can you imagine dealing with the same issue for not twelve *months* but twelve long *years*? She tried to work it out herself to no avail and no one else would even touch her, let alone help her. She was bent over with pain, guilt, and shame. She felt lonely, abandoned, rejected, and misunderstood. But when she saw her Jesus, she did not allow any of that to keep her from reaching out to touch Him.

By this time she was desperate enough, determined enough, and bold enough to press through the crowd to reach the only One she knew could heal her sickness. Nothing would stand in the way between her and her Deliverer. When she reached out and touched Jesus, He looked at the woman and recognized all that she had gone through to reach Him. He knew that others had ostracized her and that it took great courage for her to even enter the crowds, because no one wanted to be around her. Yet in spite of her shame, she approached Jesus with humility and

INSPIRATION 11: INHALE FREEDOM

reached out to touch Him. Jesus responded and said, "Your faith has healed you." (Mathew 9:22)

You see, Jesus was moved by the infirmed woman's faith in Him. Ephesians 3:12 says that, "In him and through faith in him we may approach God with freedom and confidence." Freedom in Christ means that we can now boldly and confidently approach the throne of Grace through our faith in Jesus. Because of her faith, Jesus was moved to heal the infirmed woman and free her to live life fully.

How about you? Do you have any persistent issues that you are dealing with today? Have you been bound up by something that has you bent over with pain or even shame? Like the infirmed woman, you cannot deliver yourself—but by the grace of God, you can be set free. If you will reach out to your God in faith, He will loose you and set you free to live the life you were created to live.

Take the heavy burdens that you have been carrying around and give them to God. If you are bound up by something that you have done or something that has been done to you in the past, it is time to let it go. Forgive yourself and others, then exhale and release it.

The enemy wants to make you a prisoner of your past, but God wants you to be delivered. God wants to free you from your past and give you a bright new future. But He won't give you something new until you release the old. You cannot inhale and receive fresh new oxygen until you exhale and release the toxic carbon dioxide.

Holding on to past hurt and pain is like holding on to toxic carbon dioxide. It benefits nothing and only serves to harm you. It is time to exhale and release it so you can begin to take in something new again. While dealing with your issue, others may have judged and rejected you, but God will never leave you nor forsake you. If you will only reach out and touch Him, you will then be able to receive liberation from God so you can live the life you were created to live.

It is time to exhale and release anything that has been holding you back from becoming all that God created you to be. Let go of every negative thought, toxic emotion, and self-sabotaging habit that is binding and keeping you from living life fully. God wants to liberate your spirit. He wants to free you from all anger, pain, hatred, and self-loathing.

Open up and allow God to breathe into your spirit. Allow Him to fill you with His power, peace, and joy. Accept God's grace and mercy and let His love flow freely into every area of your life. The more you release those things that are binding you, the more you will begin to experience God's freedom. Living life with no boundaries is closer than you think. Just Breathe. Your life of real freedom in Christ is just a breath away.

INSPIRATION 12:
Inhale Humility

Developing Your Servant's Heart

For even the Son of Man did not come to be served, but to serve, and to give his life as a ransom for many.
(MARK 10:45)

In the previous chapter, we inhaled freedom. In this chapter, we will begin to flow and grow with God's inspired Word on **humility** and begin developing a servant's heart.

I realize that humility may not be a characteristic that many seek to develop. Love, hope, faith, and joy are probably much more sought after. All of the things that humility represents—self-denial, suffering, sacrifice, and submission—are unpopular to the world.

In a culture that promotes self-ambition, self-interests, power, and authority, humility seems like a foreign concept. We would much rather proclaim our rights in Christ and declare our freedom as we did in the previous chapter. But we must be careful that we don't confuse our freedom *in* Christ with freedom *from* Christ.

Yes, we have been released from the bondage of sin and are no longer bound by law. Under the new covenant, we live under grace and freely enjoy the benefits of being a child of the Most High God. Before Christ delivered us, we were slaves to sin. We lived under the old law of Moses and our service was to the letter of the law. People offered up sacrifices and participated in rites and ceremonies according to the law.

But now, under the Gospel, we have been delivered from that law. We have been set free to worship God in spirit and truth (see John 4:24). The worship required by the Gospel is far different from that required by the law. We no longer worship according to the letter of the law but based on the spirit and the heart. Worship under the law did not produce a renewing of the heart. The Jews carried out many rituals and offered up many sacrifices, but they did not lead to a change in heart. Works of the flesh produce nothing, but the Spirit gives life (see John 6:63). Service under the new Gospel is spiritual and is offered up from the heart.

FREE TO SERVE

But now, by dying to what once bound us, we have been released from the law so that we serve in the new way of the Spirit, and not in the old way of the written code. (Romans 7:6)

God delivered us from the law that we may serve Him in newness of the Spirit. Under the new covenant, God's law is written into our hearts (see Hebrews 8:10). Today, we are no longer living under the bondage of the law, but we willingly serve God in spirit and truth.

But freedom in Christ does not mean freedom to live according to our own will. We are no longer slaves to sin (our wills), but we are servants to God (His will). As God's servants, we are not at liberty to indulge in those things that would dishonor Him.

We are not to live in contempt of the laws of God and men. Christians are not to abuse their freedom in Christ and take God's grace for granted. Remember, you do not belong to yourself. You were bought with a great price. Therefore, you are to honor God with your body. (See 1 Corinthians 6:20)

You, my brothers, were called to be free. But do not use your freedom to indulge the sinful nature; rather, serve one another in love.
(GALATIANS 5:13)

We are called to serve one another in love and are now living under the law of love where we look out for the welfare of others. We are called to put aside our own selfish ambitions, self-centered thoughts, and self-seeking motives and are to root out jealousy, envy, and our lust for power.

As Christians, we are called to unite in love, support one another, and meet each other's needs. When we serve each other, we are humbly submitting ourselves in loving service to our Heavenly Father. Jesus had an enormous love and compassion for people, and He modeled humility and service throughout His entire ministry. We need not look any further than His example to understand what God expects of us. God chose to bring Jesus into this world under humble circumstances, and throughout His life, humility continued to be the hallmark of Jesus' ministry.

INSPIRATION 12: INHALE HUMILITY

JESUS CAME TO SERVE

Your attitude should be the same as that of Christ Jesus: Who, being in very nature God, did not consider equality with God something to be grasped, but made Himself nothing, taking the very nature of a servant, being made in human likeness. And being found in appearance as a man, he humbled himself and became obedient to death—even death on a cross! (Philippians 2:5-8)

From the beginning, Jesus humbled Himself and put aside His divine nature to take on the human nature of man. He did not cling to the fact that He Himself was One with God. He willingly came down from Heaven and gave up His glory to become a mere man. He could have been born into a rich family and had servants waiting on Him day and night, but, instead, He was born in a lowly manger to a couple who lived a humble life.

Jesus stripped Himself of all glory and honor and made Himself nothing, so that one day He would become our everything. Jesus was God, the Creator of the universe. The Creator chose to take on the likeness of His creation so He could set us free to live life eternally. Jesus came to earth to do the will of His Father and carry out His great plan of salvation. His life and ministry was about love, humility, and service.

He did not come to earth to be served, but instead to serve (see Mark 10:45). Service was so important to Him that He modeled this for His disciples when He washed their feet (see John 13:14). After Jesus had washed their feet, He told them that they were to do the same for one another. Jesus was not asking them to literally wash each other's feet, but rather follow

His example of humility. God wanted them to develop a spirit of humility and lovingly serve one another.

As Christians, when we see an opportunity to meet a need, we should move to meet it. Jesus did not consider Himself to be above any menial act of service and neither should we. Throughout the Bible, we see example after example where Jesus served in places that others would not. He loved the unlovable; He touched the untouchable; and He reached out to minister to those whom others had rejected. Jesus taught His disciples what it truly meant to follow Him.

Then Jesus said to his disciples, "If anyone would come after me, he must deny himself and take up his cross and follow me."
(MATHEW 16:24)

Truly, following God means denying yourself. Put aside your selfish desires and follow God's will for your life. God is calling you to be less self-centered and become more Christ-centered. When you follow Jesus' example of humility, you learn to put aside your needs to meet the needs of others.

If you are operating in an "it's all about me" mentality, you fail to consider the needs of others—you only think about your own desires and ways to advance your own agenda. You won't do anything for the benefit of others that is inconvenient or makes you uncomfortable. But, as you mature in Christ and develop a heart of humility, you will be willing to sacrifice and suffer in your ministry to others.

Jesus made the ultimate sacrifice and endured unimaginable suffering and pain on the cross for us. That cross represents humility, sacrifice, suffering, and death. Jesus willingly gave up

INSPIRATION 12: INHALE HUMILITY

His life that we may live. No one took His life from Him. He was still God and could have come down from the cross if He chose to do so, but He stayed on the cross and endured the great pain so His Father's will would be done.

> *"Father, if you are willing, take this cup from me; yet not my will, but yours be done."*
> (LUKE 22:42)

If you are going to follow God, be willing to pick up your cross, which means laying down your flesh. Our flesh is selfish, self-serving, full of pride, and only seeks to meet its own desires. Submitting to God's will is challenging because it goes against our very nature.

We must crucify our flesh each day as we daily make a decision to follow God. Answer this question each day: "Will I follow the world or will I follow God?" Jesus was willing to give up His life to carry out God's master plan. Are you willing to let go of your life to pick up your cross and follow Him?

The Bible says that, "The man who loves his life will lose it, while the man who hates his life in this world will keep it for eternal life." (John 12:25) God wants you to love serving Him more than you love your life. Will you allow God to interrupt your plans for His purposes?

So many people today are caught up in their own pursuit of happiness. They have high hopes, goals, and dreams that are not aligned to God's purposes. God has great plans for you. He plans to prosper and promote you...but you must do it His way, not your way.

Psalm 18:30 tells us that God's way is perfect. Following God means giving up your need to have everything your way and being willing to do things His way. He will require you to sacrifice and suffer sometimes for the benefit of others, but His purpose is far greater than your plans. If you would just submit to Him and follow His will, God could minister to many others through your life—and submitting to God requires that we crucify our flesh and lay down our pride.

PUT ASIDE YOUR PRIDE

Young men, in the same way be submissive to those who are older. All of you, clothe yourselves with humility toward one another, because, "God opposes the proud but gives grace to the humble."
(1 PETER 5:5)

God wants us to cover ourselves in humility and live in loving service to one another. If you are proud and think more highly of yourself than you ought to, you won't have the heart to serve God and others. Your service to God must be led by your heart. God is not only interested in what you do, but He is also interested in the motivation behind what you do—so make sure that your service is led by your heart.

You must have genuine love and compassion for others. You should look not only to your own interests, but also to the interests of others. (See Philippians 2:4)

Pride makes us self-centered, and self-centered people are motivated by their desires. The desires of selfish people vary, but usually they involve relentless pursuit of more money, possessions, power, higher status, and recognition. Selfish ambition to advance your own agenda without regard of others is in complete opposition to God's will for your life. If you want to be honored by God, lay down your pride and humble yourself before Him. Proverbs warns us that a heart full of pride leads to a man's downfall.

> *Before his downfall a man's heart is proud,*
> *but humility comes before honor.*
> (PROVERBS 18:12)

YOU CAN'T DO IT ON YOUR OWN

Pride deceives us into believing in our own abilities. As we experience more success, we begin to believe that all we have accumulated and accomplished was in our own strength. But John 15:5 tells us that we can do nothing outside of Christ: "I am the vine, you are the branches. He who abides in Me, and I in him, bears much fruit; for without Me you can do nothing."

It is only by the grace and power of God that you are able to do what you do and have what you have, so do not boast of your own accomplishments, but instead acknowledge God at all times. God tells us that we are not to boast about our own wisdom, strength, or riches but to boast about our loving Lord who gives us the grace to accomplish such things. (see Jeremiah 9:23-24)

Paul gladly boasted about his weaknesses so Christ's power could rest upon him. Paul recognized that God's strength was made perfect in his weakness (2 Corinthians 12:9). If you are full of pride and believe that you are strong on your own, the power of God will not rest upon you. God will allow you to go it alone and try to accomplish something without His help. It is only when you humble yourself and admit that you can do nothing without Him that God will pick you up and show you the Way. God's grace and anointing is on those who acknowledge that they need His grace. When you take your confidence out of yourself and put it in your God, He will begin to do a mighty work in and through you.

HUMBLE AS A CHILD

Jesus used many opportunities to teach His disciples about humility. At one such time, the disciples had approached Jesus and asked Him who would be the greatest in the kingdom of heaven. They were jockeying for a position in the Kingdom that Jesus was setting up. The disciples had become self-centered and instead of seeking a place of service, they sought positions of power.

Jesus used this opportunity to teach them a lesson about humility. He called forth a little child and had him stand before them. And he said: "I tell you the truth, unless you change and become like little children, you will never enter the kingdom of heaven (Mathew 18:3). We are *not* to be *childish* like the disciples were, arguing over petty things. But we *are* to be *childlike*, taking on a heart of humility and sincerity.

Children, when very young, do not desire authority, power, and position. They submit to their parents' authority and are teachable. Children are willingly dependent on their parents and put all of their trust in them. God is calling on us to become simple and humble, as little children, and willing to be the least of all. Rather than seeking worldly ambition or power, children act as if all are equal. We must daily examine our own spirits and pray for a heart of humility.

INSPIRATION 12: INHALE HUMILITY

GOD'S LEADERS SERVE

We've all heard the saying, "Be careful what you ask for." Jesus was in effect saying this to His disciples when two of them approached Him about obtaining a top position in His Kingdom. The other ten were upset because they wanted the top position for themselves. "You don't know what you are asking," Jesus said to them. "Can you drink from the cup I am going to drink?" (Mathew 20:22). Jesus went on to say that whoever wanted to be great among them must be their servant and whoever wanted to be first must be their slave (Mathew 20:26-27).

In the world system, leaders command others to serve them but in God's system, leaders are to serve others. God's concept of leadership is radically different from that of the world. Let's take a look at some of the differences between the world's system of leadership and God's system.

World's System	*God's System*
Comfort	Discomfort, suffering
Convenience	Inconvenience, sacrifice
Pride	Humility
Selfish	Selfless
Authority	Submission
Others serving you	You serving others
Self-centered	Christ-centered
You are exalted	God is exalted

If you want to be a leader in God's Kingdom, humble yourself to serve your followers. God's way of leading requires a humble spirit and a servant's heart. After the disciples learned what was truly required of a leader in God's Kingdom, they may have reconsidered their request. Even after following Jesus and learning from Him, they still did not fully understand what it meant to drink from His cup.

Jesus' entire life was given for ministering to others. He provided for their needs, denied Himself for them, and was about to lay down His life for them. Jesus was preparing for the ultimate sacrifice of giving up His life to rescue man from the grips of sin. He was willing to give up His life so that others might have life. It is in this spirit of humility, service, and sacrifice that He was teaching His disciples to operate.

Today, we must each examine our own motives for serving in God's Kingdom. Are we doing it out of true love and compassion for people? Or are we seeking power, position, rewards, and recognition? Are you willing to put aside your comforts to meet someone else's needs? Are you willing to sacrifice and suffer for the benefit of others? Do you sit back and wait to be served or do you go out and seek ways to serve others?

God wants you to see a need and then move to meet it, period. Stepping up to be a leader in God's Kingdom requires stepping down from your ego. Having a high position in the Kingdom of God requires a higher level of service. Serve because you have the heart to serve even when no one is watching and it seems to go unnoticed. God notices every good deed you do for His children. If you will honor Him, He will be careful to honor you.

As you exhale to release pride, selfishness, and self-centeredness, you will open up to allow God's spirit of humility to

INSPIRATION 12: INHALE HUMILITY

enter into your life. As you give up your need for control and allow God to have His way in your life, you will become more humble like Christ and develop a passion for helping people. You are closer to it than you may believe. Just Breathe. Your life of humility and loving service that glorifies your Heavenly Father is just a breath away.

INSPIRATION 13:
Inhale Balance

Centering Your Life Around What Matters Most

But seek ye first the kingdom of God, and his righteousness; and all these things shall be added unto you.
(MATHEW 6:33 KJV)

In the previous chapter, we inhaled humility. In this chapter, we will begin to flow and grow with God's inspired Word on **balance**.

As twenty-first century women, we have many competing priorities in our lives. Today, we live in a much more fast-paced society than our ancestors did. Technology advances such as cell phones, email, and the Internet set us up to feel that we must be constantly connected and available at all times. We must deal with the demands of our family, home, job, church, friends, and parents. Our To-Do lists are overflowing and no matter how much we do, there's always more to be done. We often end our days feeling exhausted and unfulfilled, as if we have accomplished nothing.

In trying to juggle all of the balls that we have in the air at the same time, we can become stressed and overwhelmed. We feel off-balance and we don't know how to get harmony back

INSPIRATION 13: INHALE BALANCE

into our lives. We strive to be productive like the Proverbs 31 woman, but the never-ending demands on our time become too much to bear. In this hurried society, we have many more things to do, but the same twenty-four hours each day to get them done. How do we find balance in it all?

To answer this question, we must turn to God. When you seek God first in everything you do, everything else will begin to fall into place (see Mathew 6:33). You must make Jesus the center of your life. When Jesus is not at the core of your life, it's easy for things to spiral quickly out of control. You may begin to feel anxious, off-center, and imbalanced.

Living a life of balance is not easy to do in this day and age, but you have a much better chance of accomplishing it when you turn your To-Do list over to God. Pray and ask God to examine the activities that you give your time and attention to. Ask Him to help you make the necessary changes to bring order back to your life. Look to God to help you prioritize your projects and commitments according to what He knows you should be focused on.

MANAGE YOUR TIME WISELY

The simple matter of the truth is that time is limited. Come to understand that time is your most valuable resource. Learning how to manage your time effectively is crucial to living a balanced life. There are only twenty-four hours in a day, so you do not have an unlimited supply of time to get things done. That being the case, it is wise to conclude that you cannot do everything.

As natural caretakers, women often try to be everything to everyone. We find it difficult to say "no" and set real boundaries in our relationships with others. If you are going to complete your divine assignment and live out your purpose and mission in life, you simply cannot be everything to everyone. God did not send you here to do all things.

He has placed you on this earth with a particular purpose and you have a divine assignment. God will anoint you to become all He created you to be and do what He has called you to do. You will struggle to gain a sense of balance if you keep trying to do things outside of God's will for your life.

WHAT MATTERS MOST TO YOU?

Before you can set out to achieve life balance, you must get clear about your purpose and mission in life. The answer to the meaning of your life can only be found in God. With the help of the Holy Spirit, you need to define your core values and those things that matter most to you. From there, you can create a clear and compelling vision for your life that will guide you when making choices about how to spend your time.

When your purpose, mission, and core values are clearly defined, it becomes easier to look at your To-Do list and see what changes must be made. Based on what you decide is important to you, what changes do you need to make?

Some things on your To-Do list may need to move up to the top while others may need to move down. Some things may need to be added while others need to be removed altogether.

INSPIRATION 13: INHALE BALANCE

Taming your To-Do list is a job in and of itself and you may not have the emotional energy to get through it. It is difficult to come to terms with the fact that you are not superwoman and you cannot do everything. You will need the ongoing help of the Holy Spirit as you make these very important changes.

If your core values indicate that family is important to you but from looking at the way you spend your time, you see that you are not carving out much time for family activities, you need to make some changes. If starting your own business is important to you, but you are not spending even fifteen minutes a day towards that effort, then it's time to make some adjustments.

If you look at your list and see that a vast amount of time is spent towards activities that add little or no value to your life, it's time to do something differently.

THE PRESENT IS A GIFT

I have a prayer that I say when I wake up every morning, "Thank you, God, for today because today is the present and the present is a gift. Please help me to use my present to be productive and make progress towards my promised land." Each and every day that we wake up is a blessing. It is the most precious present and treasure we have on earth. The present is just that—we can only use it in the here-and-now. Once today is over, it's over. We have to make the most of each day that has been granted to us.

Make sure that you are making the most of your time and using it to help you move forward towards accomplishing your goals. Remember that your promised land is the vision you have for your life. Are you using your presents to make progress towards your promised land? Prioritize your To-Do list with those activities that are going to help you make the most progress in moving closer to where you want to be in life.

Accept that you will have to say "no" to some things in order to say "yes" to others. You may be doing some good things, but they may not be the things God has led you to do. It may be good work, but the question is, "Is it the *right* work for you to be doing at this time in your life?"

Be willing to put everything on the table and examine it in light of your purpose, mission and core values. Only then will you be on your way to living a more balanced life.

BE WILLING TO LET SOME THINGS GO

Moving towards a more balanced and centered life is an ongoing process. As you encounter circumstances beyond your control and enter different seasons of your life, what matters most to you at one moment may change in the next. For example, let's say one of your core values is to invest in yourself, so you decide to go back to college to get a higher degree.

While focused on your education, one of your parents suddenly becomes ill and dependent upon you for care. What do you do in this situation? Because family is an important core value for you, you may decide to temporarily stop attending college so you can step in and be there for your parent.

You can always go back to college—and you should as soon it is reasonable to do so—but this is an opportunity to honor your parent and show the love that has always been shown to you. If you can successfully juggle attending college and caring

INSPIRATION 13: INHALE BALANCE

for your parent while also working and caring for your children and home, then, by all means, do so. But if you know it will be too much, it is better to make the decision to put your degree temporarily on hold so you don't stretch yourself too thin.

These are the types of challenges we face on a regular basis and what makes maintaining balance seem so elusive. We stress ourselves out when we try to take on too much at one time. When we finally break under the weight of it all and have to admit that we need to let some things go, we beat ourselves up and feel like failures.

"I can do all things through Christ who strengthens me" is an often-quoted Scripture—I often call upon it myself (see Philippians 4:13). But understand that it is not saying that you can literally do *every* and *any* thing. The strength to do the things you do comes through Christ.

God is not going to strengthen you to do everything under the sun; He is going to enable you to do *the things He has called you to do*. This is why it is so important that you first seek God in everything you do—you need to make sure that what you are doing is what *God* wants you to be doing during this season in your life. Because your strength comes from Him, you need to be certain that the activities on your To-Do list are the things He wants you to get done. God will anoint you and provide you the grace to do what He has called you to do.

MAKE TIME FOR SELF-CARE

As women, we find it easy to take care of others, but we often neglect taking care of ourselves. Exercise, long hot bubble baths, meditation with God, reading the Bible, and prayer often get pushed off the list because we feel we simply don't have the time. We are so busy taking care of others and tending to a variety of demands that we consider more pressing. At the end of the day, we find that there is no room left for ourselves.

We often don't even take the time for full, deep breaths that are effective in calming us down. Let's try that now. Inhale and breathe in as fully, deeply, and as long you can. Now exhale and breathe out slowly and for as long as you can.

Notice that after you have fully emptied your lungs, your body automatically inhales to draw in a fresh new breath of oxygen. God set it up this way. We inhale then exhale. Inhale again, exhale again. It is a rhythmic, balanced process of releasing what you no longer need to make room to receive what you do need.

Our lives follow this same principle. You cannot expect to continually give to others without being replenished and restored yourself. Put yourself in the position to receive what you need so you can be in the best position to give and care for others. When you continually neglect yourself and put off those things that will reenergize and restore your mind, body, and soul, you throw your life out of balance and off-center.

You must come to realize that self-care is not selfish. If you do not take the time to take care of you, then you will not be in the best position to tend to others. If you are depleted, weary, and running on empty, what will you have to give? It is imperative that you learn to take care of yourself spiritually, mentally, emotionally, and physically. Set aside time to spend in God's presence. Read the Word, recite the Word, and meditate on

INSPIRATION 13: INHALE BALANCE

His Word daily. It will give you the nourishment you need to accomplish the tasks beforehand.

Many women feel guilty when they take out time for themselves. When they have to turn down someone's request for a demand on their time, they may feel anxious and uneasy, because we don't like to let others down. If I am describing you, let's look at the story of two sisters in the Bible, Martha and Mary.

ARE YOU A MARTHA OR A MARY?

Martha graciously volunteered to host a dinner for Jesus and His disciples at her home. Martha was busy working in the kitchen and trying to keep up with serving the guests but her younger sister, Mary, was sitting down. Mary was intrigued with Jesus' teachings and she was listening to Him intently.

Martha, out of frustration that Mary was not helping her, approached Jesus with her concerns. She wanted Jesus to tell Mary to get up and help her serve. But instead of rebuking Mary, Jesus gently corrected Martha.

> "Martha, Martha," the Lord answered, "you are worried and upset about many things, but only one thing is needed. Mary has chosen what is better, and it will not be taken away from her."
> (LUKE 10:41-42)

Jesus appreciated Martha's service, but He pointed out that Mary had made a better choice. While Martha was focused on providing for the guests' physical needs, Mary was tending to her own spiritual needs. Martha was serving food for their bodies, but Mary was receiving food for her soul. Mary recognized that it was not every day that she could sit in the presence of her Lord and receive a word from Him. She seized the opportunity to hear God's Word and build up her faith in Him.

In today's fast-paced society, we all have busy schedules and many things on our to-do-lists. But do not get so distracted with your daily duties that you forsake sitting down in God's presence to be renewed by His Word. If you keep running around like Martha, trying to be everything to everyone, you will only wear yourself out.

Please do not misunderstand the message here. Jesus was not encouraging laziness. We should be productive and get things done. Mary was not sitting simply to get out of work. She was sitting in God's presence to be strengthened by His Word. As women of God, we must realize that we must take out time to be replenished by God's Word. If you are going to stay strong and be in the position to care for your family, you must first tend to your own needs.

It's time to take your self-care more seriously. It is not healthy to be working continuously and not taking a break. Make time each day for some kind of "me time." I like to take long, hot bubble baths as often as I can and to read and meditate on God's Word. Do whatever works for you. Find out what inspires you and carve out a quiet place in your home to relax at the end of each day.

It is time to let go of the need to please others and the stress that accompanies a lifestyle of trying to be everything to everyone. Now is the time to release anxiety and accept the fact that

INSPIRATION 13: INHALE BALANCE

you cannot accomplish all things at once. Starting today, you will make self-care a priority in your life and inhale restoration and relaxation. You will breathe in a new life that is centered around your purpose, mission, and core values—those things that matter most. Your more centered, life of balance is closer than you think. Just breathe. A more fulfilling, balanced life is just a breath away.

INSPIRATION 14:
Inhale Wisdom

Becoming Wiser with God's Discerning Word

> *Wisdom is supreme; therefore get wisdom. Though it cost all you have, get understanding.*
> (Proverbs 4:7)

In the previous chapter, we inhaled balance. In this chapter, we will begin to flow and grow with God's inspired Word on **wisdom**.

King Solomon is most well known for his vast wisdom. The book of Proverbs (believed to have been written by Solomon) is filled with words of wisdom to guide your daily walk in Christ. Solomon obtained this great wisdom because he asked for it. God gave him an opportunity to ask for anything he wanted.

Solomon could have asked for riches and wealth or he could have requested the most beautiful lady in the land. Instead, he made the wiser choice and asked for wisdom and understanding (see 2 Chronicles 1:7-12). God was moved by Solomon's request and granted it to him. As a result, not only did he gain understanding, but he also attained wealth and riches.

INSPIRATION 14: INHALE WISDOM

Solomon understood that wisdom is the foundation for everything. Without an understanding of God's Word, His will, and His way for your life, you will be lost in darkness. Unless you come to truly know Christ and the salvation that is found only in Him, you will remain trapped in your own ignorance. Jesus is the Word made flesh and the Word is the Truth (see John 1:14) It is our job to seek out the Truth so we may live our lives according to it. God's Word will light up your path in the midst of the dark world in which we live.

> *Your word is a lamp to my feet and a light for my path.*
> (PSALM 119:105)

SEEK GOD'S WISDOM DILIGENTLY

Those who do not know the Word will walk around in darkness and confusion and eventually stumble and fall. God's Word is like a lamp that can be carried in the hand of the believer. As you journey through this dark world, carry your light with you wherever you go. It will guide you and keep you from veering off onto the wrong path. The Word will keep you walking upright and moving forward in the right direction. Are you lacking godly wisdom in your life today? If so, take a lesson from Solomon and just ask for it.

> *If any of you lacks wisdom, he should ask God, who gives generously to all without finding fault, and it will be given to him.*
> (JAMES 1:5)

God will grant you knowledge and understanding if you seek it diligently in Him. Do whatever it takes and pay whatever price you must in order to obtain wisdom (see Proverbs 4:7). Be willing to spend time searching and studying the Scriptures to gain true understanding.

GODLY WISDOM VERSUS WORLDLY WISDOM

Solomon was dedicated and diligent in seeking out God's wisdom. As you seek wisdom, make sure you are seeking *godly* wisdom and not worldly wisdom. The world's way is far different and inferior to God's way. Don't be content to do what everyone else is doing.

The only thing that matters is doing what God's Word says is the right thing to do. Man's way is foolishness to God. We are to walk in God's wisdom and do things His way. If you want to become wise, turn over your thoughts and your mind to God.

> *Stop deceiving yourselves. If you think you are wise by this world's standards, you need to become a fool to be truly wise.*
> (1 Corinthians 3:18 NLT)

LET GOD REPROGRAM YOUR MIND

True wisdom comes from God and is not of this world. Be willing to humble yourself and put aside your worldly wisdom to open up and receive God's wisdom. As long as you think you already know it all, God will not be able to teach you. A fool thinks he already has all the answers.

He would rather hear himself speak than listen to the advice and counsel of others. God wants you to realize that living life according to the world's standards is foolish and will profit you nothing. Do not boast about your education, your degrees, or your street smarts. None of those things is of much importance

INSPIRATION 14: INHALE WISDOM

to God. The most pressing issue is getting to know God's Word and His will for your life. God's way is radically different from the world's way, so you must reprogram your mind to think the way He thinks.

> *"For my thoughts are not your thoughts, neither are your ways my ways," declares the LORD.*
> (ISAIAH 55:8)

You have to submit your mind unto God so He can renew it and give you a new way of thinking. You will never come to truly know Christ with the world's way of thinking. You must believe with your heart and not with your mind. The mysteries of the world belong to God and man's mind does not have the capacity to understand it all.

When you try to make sense of it using worldly logic, you will only become confused. Abandon your worldly way of thinking to align your thoughts with God's way of thinking. As we see in Romans, God wants to radically renew your mind and make you into who He created you to be:

> *Do not conform any longer to the pattern of this world, but be transformed by the renewing of your mind. Then you will be able to test and approve what God's will is—his good, pleasing and perfect will.*
> (ROMANS 12:2)

If you desire to pattern your mind after Christ, you must focus it on those things that are pure, righteous, and true:

> *Finally, brothers, whatever is true, whatever is noble, whatever is right, whatever is pure, whatever is lovely, whatever is admirable—if anything is excellent or praiseworthy—think about such things.*
> (PHILIPPIANS 4:8)

Be careful to meditate on God's Word day and night so you can begin to think about things in a fresh, new way. You are responsible for studying the Word for yourself (see 2 Timothy 2:15). It's important to study the Word, but you cannot do it on your own. Man can read the Bible from Genesis to Revelation and still walk away confused and in darkness. As a believer, you must humbly pray and ask God to enlighten you and reveal the truth to you in a way that you will understand it.

The Holy Spirit dwells within you so you have immediate access to divine wisdom at all times. Learn how to draw upon that wisdom and put it to work in your life. The true wisdom that you should seek is not the way of the world, but the full knowledge of God. Come to know Jesus as your Lord and Savior; He is your only way to eternal life with God.

THE WISE ANT

> *Go to the ant, you sluggard; consider its ways and be wise! It has no commander, no overseer or ruler, yet it stores its provisions in summer and gathers its food at harvest.*
> (PROVERBS 6:6-8)

The ant is one of the smallest creatures and we consider it to be weak, yet it is wiser than many men. Without any guidance or supervision, ants preserve and protect themselves. With a wise eye to the future, they work diligently in the summer and store up all they can for harder times. During the fall and spring, they

INSPIRATION 14: INHALE WISDOM

live underground and eat off their savings from the summer. They are still able to prosper during tough times, because they saved wisely when times were good.

This nation has been facing some tough times for the past few years and economists predict that our tough days are not going to be over anytime soon. I've shared with you how I have had more than my fair share of layoffs over this past decade. I have seen my income disappear and then reappear at a much lower wage than what I was earning prior to the recession.

My housing value has dropped and my retirement savings in the stock market have plummeted. Despite all of that, I never missed a house payment or car payment because of one major thing that I did right before the recession. I am sure that you've heard about emergency savings countless times.

Financial planners always advise that you save at least three months' worth of your expenses in case of a layoff or some other emergency that interrupts your income flow. This money should be liquid cash that you can get your hands on quickly when times get tough.

When I was working and earning a great income, I consistently saved and built up my emergency fund to cover two years of expenses. Did you hear me? Not three months…two years. As a result, I did not have to panic like others did when I was laid off. I trusted and believed in God to provide for all my needs, and I knew that I wisely saved my money, so I gave God something to work with. That cushion really came in handy when I needed it most and that is exactly why it is so important to build up your emergency fund.

During these tough economic times, you have to work smarter, not harder. With a lack of jobs and with many jobs returning at much lower wages, it is imperative that you become wise with your money. Save all you can, when you can, so you can still eat when you can no longer work. Financial advisors now advise you to save at least six to nine months of expenses, because in this job market it takes much longer to find a job.

Just ask all the people who have been out of work for longer than two years: unemployment benefits are not enough to sustain you, and they may very well run out before you can land another job. The smartest move you can make to empower yourself is to store up as much cash as you can for navigating these difficult economic times and lowering your expenses.

THE VIRTUOUS WOMAN

The wise woman builds her house, but with her own hands the foolish one tears hers down.
(Proverbs 14:1)

Are you building your house or tearing it down? But we are not talking about a building here. The house in this verse refers to your home and your home is wherever you make it. I am talking about your family. A wise woman lives in a way that builds up her family and causes it to prosper while a foolish woman tears her family down. For an example of a wise woman, look to the virtuous woman in Proverbs. (verses10-31)

The virtuous woman had a great influence over her family. She rose early and went to bed late at night. She spent her time wisely and proved to be highly productive. She handled her money wisely and made smart investments that paid off

INSPIRATION 14: INHALE WISDOM

greatly. She managed her household efficiently and left nothing undone. She worked diligently in the fields with her hands and demonstrated tremendous strength.

The virtuous woman directed the care of her children and made sure that her household always had food on the table. She was compassionate and reached out her hands to the poor. The virtuous woman feared and praised the Lord and made Him the Head of her life. Living your life with this type of wisdom is what is needed to build up your family and cause it to prosper for generations to come.

Do not be foolish and go out spending money you don't have on things you cannot afford. Now, more than ever, is the time to be smart and live within your means. The virtuous woman also teaches us to be wise with our time. A wise woman realizes that there is much to be done. She does not sit around lazily watching television all day and gossiping with her friends as if she has nothing to do.

She wakes up early and goes to bed late and is highly productive in between. She prioritizes her time around what matters most and does what is needed to get the job done. If you are a mother, your most important and urgent job at hand is raising your kids. It is often said that kids do not come with a book—that there is no instruction manual on how to effectively raise kids. I believe you do have a book that you can turn to when seeking answers to questions concerning your kids. The Bible is filled with divine wisdom for all matters concerning you as a mother.

It is time to wise up and become the woman of wisdom God created you to be. Now is the time to exhale and let go of ignorance and foolish mindsets. The Bible states that people perish because of lack of knowledge (see Hosea 4:6). If you want to live a thriving and fulfilling life, it is time to release your pride and become humble before God. He won't help you if you foolishly think you already know everything. All you have to do is ask God, trusting, and He will lead you in the understanding that you need for every area of your life. Take a deep breath now and start breathing in the wisdom of God. His divine wisdom dwells within you and is abundantly available whenever you need it. Becoming a wiser woman is closer than you think. Just breathe. Your divine wisdom is just a breath away.

INSPIRATION 15:
Inhale Confidence
Believing You Have What It Takes

I can do all things through Christ which strengtheneth me.
(Philippians 4:13 KJV)

In the previous chapter, we inhaled wisdom. In this chapter, we will begin to flow and grow with God's inspired Word on **confidence**.

The verse above is a very popular one that is often quoted, but I have found that people are quick to quote Scriptures even if they don't really believe the truth for themselves. Do you truly believe that you can do all things through Christ? For Christians, *self*-confidence is actually trusting God to enable you to do whatever it is that He has called you to do. Your confidence is not in your abilities, but instead, it is in your God. You know beyond a shadow of a doubt that nothing is impossible with God. It is a strong belief that with the help of the Holy Spirit, there is nothing you can't do.

You are secure in who you are because you know Whose you are. This type of confidence is completely founded upon your faith in God. It is authentic confidence that is rooted in the

INSPIRATION 15: INHALE CONFIDENCE

truth of God's Word and the faith you place in Him. This type of confidence is permanent and lasting, and it is the confidence that we seek as Christians. God's Word is true and with God, nothing is impossible. (see Luke 1:37)

We quote Scriptures like this regularly, but living them out in our daily lives is another matter altogether. When it comes to putting these Scriptures into practice, Ms. Insecurity rears her ugly head and steals the confidence we thought we had. Despite what the Word tells us, the contrary messages the world sends us trip us up.

Everywhere you turn, there is a message telling you that you are not smart enough, talented enough, pretty enough, or financially successful enough to get the job done. We see images on magazine covers, television, advertisements and other media that continuously inform us that we are not enough.

If you are not careful, eventually you will start buying into those lies. Slowly, but surely, you start to believe the world more than you believe the Word. Those seeds of doubt begin to take root and the fruit of insecurity and low self-esteem sprout up and take over your life. The only way to conquer those lies is to overcome them with God's Truth.

Search the Scriptures, meditate on them, and pray and ask God to renew your mind with His Word. You need to forget what the world says about you and focus on what God's Word says about you. Even with all your shortcomings, you are perfectly imperfect to God. God's strength is made perfect in your weakness (2 Corinthians 12:9). Whatever you are lacking, God will pick up the slack.

CIRCUMSTANTIAL CONFIDENCE

Too often, our culture convinces us to put our confidence in the wrong things. We are told that if we look a certain way, then we can feel good about ourselves. If we earn a certain academic degree, then we can be sure that we are intelligent enough. If we hold a certain position, then we can find security in our power.

If we live in a prestigious neighborhood and drive a certain car, then we've made it. If we have a certain amount of money, then we never have to worry about anything. If we can snag a successful man, then we can feel confident in ourselves.

The problem with all of the things that I've just named is they are temporal and circumstantial. What happens if the degree you earned no longer holds value in the job market? What happens if your beauty fades and the man walks out? What happens if you get laid off, the house gets foreclosed, and your bank account shrinks? If your confidence is tied to these things, then if they go away, so goes your so-called confidence.

I say "so-called" confidence because it is *not* the authentic confidence that we want to inhale and draw into our spirits. That type of confidence offers you a false sense of security that will not stand when it is tested by the right set of circumstances. The confidence we seek is rooted and firmly founded in God and cannot be taken from us, regardless of our circumstances.

STOP COMPETING AND COMPARING

Too many people get caught up in competing and comparing and end up developing the "Keeping Up with the Jones'" mentality. They want what others have—and more. Competing

INSPIRATION 15: INHALE CONFIDENCE

to be smarter, prettier, and more successful than the next person becomes their way of life. They continually compare themselves to others to see who is most accomplished. Many go out and spend money they don't have on things they don't want in order to impress people they don't even like.

These people live in homes they can't afford because they felt that they had to buy the biggest, most beautiful home possible to impress others. A lot of women are in debt because they constantly buy things like the latest designer clothes to keep up an image of being more successful than they truly are. The accumulation of accolades, achievements, and material possessions give them a false sense of confidence. Some people attempt to build up their confidence by trying to tear down others. They have to feel as though they are better than others in order to feel better about themselves.

The type of behavior I just described is not indicative of a genuine confidence. The simple truth is that if you need to compete and compare yourself to others, you are suffering from low self-esteem and insecurity. When you have authentic confidence, you don't get caught up in trying to be better than others—you focus, instead, on being the best God created you to be.

You will always be able to find others who are smarter, prettier, more educated, and more financially well off. But seeing others doing well should not make you feel bad about yourself. When you discover who you really are in Christ, you'll come to know that you are already enough—you are talented enough, smart enough, and pretty enough. You were fearfully and wonderfully made. God molded you in your mother's womb and made you into exactly who He wanted you to be … and God does not make mistakes.

You are already fully equipped and have what it takes to do what God has anointed you to do. If you needed more beauty to do what God called you to do, He would have given you more beauty. If you needed to be smarter to complete your assignment, God would have made you smarter. If you needed to be taller to fulfill your purpose, God would have made you taller. Trust me. God has already given you the tools to be successful in life; you just have to believe it. Stop doubting yourself and start believing in what you can do through Christ, Who is the source of your strength.

YOUR NET WORTH DOES NOT DETERMINE YOUR SELF WORTH

Perhaps you are one of the millions of people around the world who has been negatively impacted by the global economic downturn. A new economy is emerging and "job security" is becoming an obsolete term. You may not believe that you have what it takes to bounce back after all of your setbacks.

Now that you can no longer depend on your job, your home equity, your credit cards, and your savings, learn to depend on your God. God is your Rock in this storm. You can rely on Him to always be there to hold you up and sustain you.

Even when it seems like you have lost everything else, you can still gain authentic confidence. Why? Because your confidence is not based on those things—instead, your confidence is found in your faith in God. The more you trust God, the

INSPIRATION 15: INHALE CONFIDENCE

more you can begin to believe in yourself and what you can accomplish with Him on your side.

It is time for you to declare that your net worth does not determine your self-worth. Though your accounts may drop in value, you remain highly valuable and worthy in God's eyes. God knows your worth more than anyone in this world, including yourself. He knows what you are made of and the great potential that He placed inside of you.

I want you to become sure of yourself and the potential God has placed within you. Your gifts and talents are treasures from God and are worth far more than rubies and pearls. No one can take from you what God has put in you. Allow God to help you develop your gifts so you can share them fully with the world. You can rest assured that the world needs what God has put in you.

In this tough economy, where good jobs are scarce, you may begin to feel that you no longer have anything to offer to this world. I have personally experienced multiple rejection letters after applying for jobs. Companies now have automated systems in place to handle the mass number of applications they receive daily. If your resumé does not match perfectly with what the computer is looking for, it is tossed out, and you receive a rejection letter politely stating that you don't have the goods to get the job done.

After receiving enough of these rejection letters, I don't care how "Christian" or how "confident" you think you are, it is easy to begin feeling inadequate and insecure. You start to question your self-worth and doubt the value you can bring to an organization.

For a brief moment in my job search, I did begin to question my value, but God quickly reminded me of the value and treasure that is in me. The companies may reject you, others may deny you, but know that God always accepts you. Though you may have received countless rejection letters, the Bible is one big acceptance letter from God to you. God accepts you, approves of you, and greatly loves you.

It is easy to lose your confidence if you focus on the rejection you receive from others. You have to learn how to exhale and release that invalidation and in its place inhale God's inspiration. God will inspire you and remind you of your true worth. Read the Word and meditate on it with the help of the Holy Spirit so you can come to realize your worth and value in Christ.

Life's uncertainties will definitely challenge your confidence. Suddenly being thrust into a single mother role due to a divorce or being widowed can certainly lead to anxiety. You may not feel confident in your new head-of-household role and feel you don't have what it takes to raise your children on your own. Job and financial insecurity may certainly lead to you feeling less secure about your ability to provide for your children. Being forced to move from your home that gave you so much pride, joy, and a sense of accomplishment can definitely cause you to question your self-worth.

In our humanity, it is easy to succumb to our emotions and begin to feel worthless when we lose things of such value. But we must learn that the greatest treasure we own is not outside of us, it is within us. Your *self*-worth is not determined by your *net* worth. The gifts, talents, and treasures that God has placed within you are still there, regardless of your financial situation. Your value is not found in what you do, who you know, or what you own. Your value is completely defined by who you are and Whose you are. In the next chapter, we will explore who you are more fully—but for now, hold on to the fact that you are fearfully and wonderfully made.

FIND SECURITY IN SERVING THE WORLD WITH YOUR GIFTS

When you have authentic confidence, you believe that you can handle whatever comes your way. Preparation, continuously honing your skills, and developing a life-long love of learning is key to gaining confidence. The skills needed to be successful in this technology-driven job market are constantly changing and you have to change along with it to keep pace and stay relevant. When you maintain a positive attitude and remain flexible and willing to learn new skills, you'll have confidence that you can get the job done.

Ask God to help you discover your true gifts and talents and then put your focus and energy into developing them. We make a mistake when we put too much emphasis on our weaknesses and don't put enough time into developing our strengths. Why waste so much time trying to become *good* at something when you can spend the same amount of time to become *great* at it? Identify the areas where you have the greatest potential and pour your time and attention into those things.

BELIEVING YOU HAVE WHAT IT TAKES

Your confidence will begin to build when you focus on the things that God has gifted you with and called you to do. When you get on the right path and pursue your purpose rather than worldly success, you'll find security in serving the world with your gifts.

I want you to take a deep breath now and exhale all insecurity, doubts, and fears. It is time to release all toxic thoughts that convince you that you are not good enough or that you don't have what it takes. Draw in a fresh breath of God's authentic confidence. Inhale and receive into your spirit the fact that you are already enough. You already have within you everything you need to succeed and fulfill your God-given purpose in life. Your life characterized by high self-esteem and Godly confidence is closer than you think. Just breathe. Your authentic confidence is just a breath away.

INSPIRATION 16:
Inhale Authenticity
Removing the Masks to Unveil the True YOU

*I praise you because I am fearfully and wonderfully made;
your works are wonderful, I know that full well.*
(PSALM 139:14)

In the previous chapter, we inhaled a fresh new breath of confidence. In this chapter, we will begin to flow and grow with **authenticity** as we deal with some of those masks and begin to pull them away to unveil the true you.

It is a lack of confidence and security in yourself that prevents you from presenting your real self to the world. Insecurity and the belief that the world will not embrace the true you is what keeps you hiding behind your masks. In an earlier chapter we inhaled freedom. There is no more bondage I can think of than being trapped in a life that does not allow you to be true to who you really are—to freely express your personality, your style, and your unique gifts and talents to the world.

Millions of people put on their invisible masks each day and transform into someone other than who they really are. After wearing those masks for so long, they began to lose sight of their true selves and forget who they are. Are you ready to get

INSPIRATION 16: INHALE AUTHENTICITY

real? Will the real you step forward? The time has come to get a fresh new breath of authenticity and start living your truth.

Then you will know the truth, and the truth will set you free.
(John 8:32)

In chapter eleven, we discovered that God's divine truth will set you free from all bondage. If you are ready to free yourself from living life captive to the many masks you wear, you must start with God's truth. As you inhale God's truth, you'll become more alive and alert to who you really are. But the key to knowing who you really are is understanding Whose you are. You are a daughter of the Most High God. You are fearfully and wonderfully made (see Psalm 139:14). You have the image of God because He created you in His own likeness. (see Genesis 1:27)

God knit you together in your mother's womb (see Psalm 139:13). Your Heavenly Father divinely designed every detail about you down to the very hairs on your head (Luke 12:7). After God created you, He took one look at His creation and declared that it was very good (see Genesis 1:31). God loves His workmanship, and when you cover it up and keep it from the world you deny others the opportunity to benefit from God's wonderful creation. You are a one-of-a-kind masterpiece, worth far more than rubies and precious jewels (see Proverbs 31:10). You are a queen in God's royal court, and it is time that you start to embrace your uniqueness and reassess your value in the Body of Christ.

IS YOUR SPIRIT SUFFOCATING?

Is your spirit suffocating and screaming for a fresh breath of air from underneath all of those masks? Now is the time to liberate your spirit and give it the freedom to express itself fully and authentically. We live in a world that is full of pretenses and false imitations. You can easily get your hands on false designer purses, clothes, jewelry, and accessories, but let me assure you, there is no value in a copy; there is only value in the original.

An original artwork designed by a master artist can be worth millions while the copies of it only go for hundreds. The value is found in the pure authentic work. Don't settle to live life as a mere copy, imitating what you see on magazine covers and television or in the lives of people you admire. If you don't do you, it won't get done.

You will never be as good at imitating others as you can at being your true self. You are a unique, one-of-a-kind masterpiece. You hold value beyond measure. Don't value others while putting yourself down. You can admire others, learn from them, and use them as your role models, but do not try to become them. Be your best self. God anoints you to become all He created you to be; He will not assist you in trying to be someone else. Take the time to uncover the value in the real you and learn how to best present it to the world.

In the past couple of years, I discovered the value and beauty in wearing my natural hair. I made a big decision to cut off my permed hair and go back to my naturally kinky roots. At a certain coming of age, many African American girls get their hair permed, which is a chemical process that straightens kinky hair. A perm makes the hair smooth, silky, and much easier to

INSPIRATION 16: INHALE AUTHENTICITY

manage, as the advertisements claim, and I had worn a perm on my hair since I was a teenager.

I had many different reasons for removing the mask and going back to my natural state, but I did not anticipate the spiritual journey it would bring about. Part of the process requires cutting off the permed hair to get back to the roots. It had been years since I had seen my natural hair, so I did not know what to expect—I felt excited and nervous all at the same time.

After getting my hair chopped off, and looking in the mirror for the first time to see my natural texture, I felt vulnerable and exposed. I no longer had the mask of smooth, silky hair to hide behind. All of the advertisements for perms have positive connotations associated with them: smooth, silky, luscious, beautiful. The subtle suggestion is that kinky, coarse, curly hair is not luscious or beautiful.

Putting a perm on my hair always seemed like the natural thing to do because that's what I had always done—and that's what most other black women I knew did. Particularly, if you worked in corporate America as I did, you felt pressured to maintain a certain image and smooth, silky hair was definitely part of that image.

Thankfully, today it is becoming much more acceptable for black women to wear their natural locks. Society is finally beginning to recognize the natural beauty of kinky, curly hair. It still is not embraced as much as it should, and you truly need authentic confidence to rock your naturally kinky hair. Some will love it and others will not. Have confidence in yourself and know that God made your hair just the way He wanted to—and afterwards He took one look at it and declared it was good!

God loves variety and black women's hair comes in many different beautiful textures. Whether or not to go natural is a personal decision you must make for yourself. It is a decision that I do not regret and I am enjoying the journey and the freedom of expression it brings. I can freely be me in this area of my life and it inspires me to express my individuality in other areas. Once you get a good taste of authenticity in one area of your life, you will hunger and thirst for more opportunities to live your truth.

WILL THE REAL MOTHER PLEASE STAND UP?

There's a story in the Bible of two women both claiming to be the mother of a baby (see 1 Kings 3:16-27). They took their case before the wise King Solomon for a judgment. Solomon called for a sword to be used to split the child in two so each woman would get one half. While the deceiving woman was content with dividing the child, the real mother cried out to save him. She would rather give the other woman her baby than have him harmed in any way.

After seeing her reaction, Solomon gave the child to the real mother. Her motherly instincts to protect her child had revealed that she was the true mother while the imposter revealed that she did not genuinely love the child. Make sure that your actions line up with who you say you are. When you say one thing but your actions prove another, you are not being authentic.

IS IT TIME TO FACE REALITY?

Living in denial and not accepting reality is another form of not being authentic. When we face major setbacks or suffer great losses, we may not know how to come to terms with our new reality. If you or someone you love is dealing with a challenging health issue, it is hard to accept the reality of your situation. If you had a substantial financial loss during a major economic downturn, you probably tried to wrap your head around your financial statements.

Maybe you've experienced a divorce and have yet to accept that the relationship is over and that you are now the head of your household. Since the housing bust in 2008, many Americans have lost their homes and others are still struggling to hold on.

Although it is natural to be in denial after a major loss, it is important to move through that stage to get to the acceptance phase where you can embrace your new reality. It is not healthy to continually deny reality and pretend as if your loss is not real. It is imperative that you take the time to mourn your loss and allow yourself to grieve.

I'll tell you a little secret about me. One of the masks I wear is the "I'm so strong" mask. I don't like for others to see me vulnerable. After we lost my sister, I wanted to be strong for everyone else. I did not cry in public and instead comforted others. I eventually had to lay down that mask and allow myself the time to properly grieve. I have experienced multiple layoffs in my career and major blows to my retirement savings. That is a lot of loss to come to terms with and it is not easy.

I went through a divorce when my son was only three years old and found myself raising my son alone. With the grace of God, my son and I are doing great, but accepting my new role and living it each day is no cake-walk.

It is important to take the time to mourn your losses, but then you must pick yourself up and move forward in your new identity. Take an honest assessment of the damage and all that you lost…then turn and look at all you have left. My new life looks far different from what I planned for it to be: I planned to still be married, but that simply is not my reality now; I definitely expected my oldest sister, Andrea, to still be with us, but God saw different; I expected to be at a certain level of retirement savings by now, but that is not my reality.

FIND YOUR TRUE IDENTITY IN CHRIST

What reality do you still need to come to terms with? Acceptance is key to your living an authentic life. Once you accept your new circumstances, you can move forward with a fresh new vision for your life. Map out where you want to go from here. You may have lost a lot, but God has much more in store for you.

Don't waste your energy rejecting what is. Accept it so you can get on with your new reality. Don't live in the past and long to have what you used to have. Look ahead to what God has in store for your new future. If you have been defining yourself by something you lost, accepting the fact that it's gone and never coming back can be especially difficult.

If you were once "Mrs." and now you are "Ms." your sense of self may be all out of whack now. If you held a certain position

INSPIRATION 16: INHALE AUTHENTICITY

and took pride in your job title, you may feel insecure now that you no longer carry that title. If you identified yourself by a certain financial status or upscale neighborhood, you may feel uneasy driving up to your new address in a different part of town.

When you no longer do what you used to do, or have what you used to have, who do you become? Who are you when the dust settles? You have an opportunity to redefine yourself now. If you have always defined yourself by external things, it's time to find your true identity in Christ. No matter what you lose in this world, who you are in Christ can never be taken from you.

You are not what you do and you are not what you have. You are who God created you to be—and God created you to be a woman of love, joy, grace, and peace. He breathed into you the spirit of strength, hope, and courage. God gave you unique gifts, talents, and personality... all to be used for His glory. When it seems that you've lost everything you thought you needed in order to have worth, that is the time when God shows you that you are worthy simply for being you.

You do not have to *do* anything or *have* anything to be valuable to God. You are loved simply for being. Drop the masks and stop pretending you still have what you used to have. Stop trying to keep up appearances and act as if nothing has changed. Accept your new reality, even if it includes a new circle of friends who genuinely love you and are not there because of what you have or what you can do for them.

Now is the time to get to the essence of who you truly are and live life from the core of you. Some may reject the new authentic you, but that's okay. Their own insecurities may keep them from embracing your new reality because it forces them to face their own.

It is time to get real, take off the masks, breathe a deep sigh of relief, exhale, and let go. Let go of trying to be someone you are not. Ditch the idea of trying to keep up false appearances to impress others. As you peel away those masks, you will begin to reveal an authentic, magnificent you. Allow God's fresh breath of authenticity to flow through your spirit and awaken the true you. Your life of truth is closer than you think. Just breathe. Your life of authenticity is just a breath away.

INSPIRATION 17:
Inhale Courage
Moving Forward in the Face of Fear

For God has not given us a spirit of fear and timidity, but of power, love, and self-discipline.
(2 Timothy 1:7 NLT)

In the previous chapter we inhaled a fresh new breath of authenticity. In this chapter, we will begin to flow and grow with God's inspired Word on **courage**.

Fear is one of the most powerful weapons the enemy uses against us in spiritual warfare. This toxic spirit is used to bind and keep us from moving forward in God's Word. When you are overcome by fear, it paralyzes you, keeps you stuck, and prevents you from pressing toward your Promised Land. Your Promised Land is that place of victory that God has shown you in a vision. It is the place where dreams are fulfilled and hopes are realized. The Promised Land represents the goals you want to accomplish and the place you want to get to in your life.

If you plan to become all God created you to be and pursue your purpose, learn how to move forward in the face of fear. Notice that you must move forward in the face of fear, not the absence of fear. It is my experience that fear is not going anywhere. Ms.

INSPIRATION 17: INHALE COURAGE

Fear is a determined spirit, and she will not simply back down. You will have to learn how to stand up to her, stare her down, and move forward anyway. You can't conquer what you won't confront, and fear is no exception to that rule.

Fear is a natural emotion we feel anytime we believe that we are not in control. God knows that we will feel fear often—this is why there are so many Scriptures that encourage us to "fear not" and "do not be afraid." God knows that we will feel the fear, but it's what we *do* with those feelings that determine whether we have courage or not.

Courage is not the absence of fear. Courage is moving forward despite the fear. Courage allows you to put your faith in God above your fear of whatever you are afraid of. In this chapter, we will focus on inhaling a fresh new breath of courage. As you exhale and release your fears, your courage slowly begins to build up and emboldens you to do what God has called you to do.

CAST DOWN THOSE FEAR-BASED THOUGHTS

Fear comes from the enemy; it is not of God. Timothy reminds us that God has given us a spirit of power, love, and self-discipline.
(2 TIMOTHY 1:7 NLT)

We must lean on the love and power of God to conquer our fears. A common acronym for fear is False Evidence Appearing Real. We know that Satan is the Prince of Lies. He loves to present things as real when they are really false.

The enemy is a master deceiver. His strategy is to fill your mind with negative thoughts and overwhelm you with "what-if" scenarios. What if I don't heal from this sickness? What if I don't find a job in time to pay my mortgage? What if I never find a loving relationship again? What if I ask for a raise and my boss fires me instead? What if I start the business I always dreamed about but it fails?

This pattern of thinking is negative and fear-based. You cannot control the thoughts that pop up in your mind, but you *can* control the thoughts you choose to dwell on. It is the enemy's job to plant those negative thoughts; it is your job to uproot them and replace them with positive thoughts that give you power.

> *Casting down arguments, and every high thing that exalts itself against the knowledge of God, and bringing into captivity every thought to the obedience of Christ.*
> (2 Corinthians 10:5 KJV)

Learn how to counter the enemy's lies with God's truths. Take every thought that is not from God and bring it under captivity. Replace those thoughts with God's truths and you will be well on your way to overcoming your fears.

FACING YOUR WORST FEARS

Fear is defined as the emotion experienced in the presence or threat of danger; courage is defined as the strength of mind to carry on in spite of danger. Again, courage is *not* the absence of fear. Acknowledge the fear and feel what you are feeling—but then make the choice to carry on in spite of it. You may think that you are very courageous, but until you are confronted by

INSPIRATION 17: INHALE COURAGE

one of your greatest fears, you won't really know what you are made of.

My sister, Daphne, was tried and tested by breast cancer back in 2007. After watching her go through that journey, I came to understand even better what my sister was made of. And let me tell you: she is made of something pretty special. I have long admired my sister for her wit, her gentle spirit, huge heart of compassion, and great passion for God. She is highly successful in her profession and greatly respected by her co-workers, family, and friends. She has always been a faithful wife, mother, sister, friend, and committed woman of God.

She's the type of person you never want to see anything bad happen to. So we were devastated when, one Sunday after dinner at my mom's, she gathered the family around the table to tell us that she had been diagnosed with breast cancer. The news came only three years after my oldest sister, Andrea, died at the young age of forty-one of sarcoidosis. So hearing this news sent a wave of fear through my family, but we united in our faith and supported my sister with words of encouragement.

I am sure that Daphne was very afraid at times. She knew full well the threat that cancer presented. But she went through her battle with grace, faith, and courage. She did everything in her power to be strong for her family. We tried to be strong for her and she was trying to be strong for us.

She sings in the choir and has a beautiful soprano voice. She loves gospel music. She used music, prayer, Scripture, her faith in God, and the support of her family and friends to pull her through. She never allowed us to do as much for her as we wanted to. As often as she could, she continued to work at her job and cook and do chores at home even as she went through chemo treatments. She refused to lie down and be beaten by the disease.

It took a lot of courage for her to get up every day and face the reality of her illness, yet still choose to keep living life fully. It seems like the more she became physically weaker, the more she became spiritually stronger. Eventually her physical strength was restored and she emerged as a stronger woman of faith because of what she had endured.

When you are facing such a frightening diagnosis and fighting the battle of your life, it's easy to lose hope and give up. Daphne refused to quit on her family and her life. She kept on living all the way through her treatments. She pushed past her fears and kept on living life as fully as her body would physically allow her to do. Eventually, her boldness and faith in God paid off. She conquered that disease and walked away with the victory. Her battle now serves as a testimony to others.

THE COURAGE OF QUEEN ESTHER

The Book of Esther in the Bible recounts a story of great courage. King Xerxes of Persia chose Esther, a young virgin, to become his queen. Esther, acting under the advice of her Uncle Mordecai, concealed her ethnicity (she was Jewish).

Later, King Xerxes' prime minister, Haman, got angry at Mordecai because Mordecai refused to bow to him. Haman plotted revenge, not only against Mordecai, but against all Jews, and tricked the King into declaring a death sentence for all Jews in the Kingdom.

INSPIRATION 17: INHALE COURAGE

Mordecai learned of the plot and asked Queen Esther to go before the King and beg for mercy for her people. Queen Esther was very afraid because she was a Jew herself and pleading for her people would put her own life at great risk. Young Queen Esther was no doubt afraid, anxious, and confused about what to do, but what Mordecai said to her next may have given her the encouragement she needed to move forward in spite of her fears.

> *If you keep quiet at a time like this, deliverance and relief for the Jews will arise from some other place, but you and your relatives will die. Who knows if perhaps you were made queen for just such a time as this.*
> (ESTHER 4:14 NLT)

Mordecai was basically telling Queen Esther that God *will* deliver His people, with or without her. Queen Esther could either be part of His great plan for deliverance or not—the choice was hers. Mordecai suggested that Esther may have been placed in the position of royalty for just such a time as this. God has a way of placing the right people in the right positions to be ready when the right opportunity arises.

After fasting and praying, Queen Esther accepted her assignment, boldly went before the King, pleaded for his mercy on her people, and was successful in her mission. The King ordered Haman to be killed in place of Mordecai. It took real guts for Queen Esther to approach the King, putting her own life in danger, but she was able to move forward because she knew God was on her side.

Will *you* have the courage to step up when God calls on you to be a part of something great? Are you willing to risk it all, step out of your comfort zone, and enter into a zone of danger to help carry out a mission for God? God has a divine purpose and a great plan for each one of us. But no one ever accomplished anything great for God by playing it safe. God's purposes will be fulfilled whether you are a part of them or not. He wants to use you in a great way, but you must be willing to trust Him and move when He says move.

What has God called you to do that requires courage? Have you been placed in the position you are in now for such a time as this? My sister, Daphne, finds herself in the position of being a breast cancer survivor. God may have allowed her to be placed in that position so she can now be an inspiration to other women confronting the same diagnosis.

God gave me the inspiration to write this book ten years ago. Within a year of getting that vision, my life, as I knew it and planned it, began to unravel. I now find myself in a new position in life. I am divorced and raising my son as a single mother. I have experienced multiple layoffs and the negative financial implications that accompanied them. But even more devastating, I lost my oldest sister, Andrea, to sarcoidosis.

I truly believe that God allowed me to be put in a position where my faith could be increased because I had to learn how to depend on Him even more than I had before. As my faith continues to grow, God has put me in a position to share His message of hope with women and children around the world. Don't minimize the position you are in now. How can God use you in that position to help fulfill His purposes?

Notice that Queen Esther fasted and prayed before she made her move. Make sure that you always go to God in prayer and wait for the Holy Spirit to guide you. Pray for God to give you a spirit of boldness and take away your fear. When you are operating within God's will, He will anoint you to do whatever it is He has appointed you to do. God will protect you and give you the victory. When He does, be sure you give Him all the glory.

GOD IS WITH YOU

After the death of Moses, God called Joshua to step up to the challenge of leading the children of Israel into the Promised Land. After giving this news to Joshua, the Lord immediately reassured him: "This is my command: be strong and courageous! Do not be afraid or discouraged. For the LORD your God is with you wherever you go." (Joshua 1:9 NLT)

God already knew that Joshua would be afraid. This is why He repeatedly encouraged Joshua and assured him that He would be with him always. In the Bible, you will find several Scriptures that command you to "fear not." God knows that in our humanity, we will feel fear, but He is commanding us not to give in to that fear.

There are all kinds of fears and phobias. You can have a fear of public speaking, a fear of heights, a fear of flying, a fear of swimming. Most people experience the feelings of fear anytime they get ready to try something new, set out to meet a new goal, or face a new challenge. The enemy particularly attacks us with the spirit of fear the moment we make up our mind to do something big for God.

Every time I made up my mind to move forward with God's vision to write this book, the enemy attacked me with the spirit of fear and I backed down. I eventually made up my mind to move forward anyway. We simply cannot escape feelings of fear, but we can take a deep breath, inhale God's spirit of courage and move forward anyway. Knowing that God is with you should give you the confidence and courage needed to conquer your fears and do all He has anointed you to do.

It is time to exhale and release all fear-based thoughts that bind you and keep you from moving forward to do what God has called you to do. God has not given you a spirit of fear. You are more than a conqueror. Open up and allow God to breathe His spirit of boldness in you. Inhale and receive the spirit of courage that allows you to conquer and confront your fears. Your courageous spirit is closer than you think. Just breathe. Your courage is just a breath away.

INSPIRATION 18:
Inhale Perseverance

Refusing to Give Up When Life Gets Tough

"Keep on asking, and you will receive what you ask for. Keep on seeking, and you will find. Keep on knocking, and the door will be opened to you."
(Mathew 7:7 NLT).

In the previous chapter, we breathed in a fresh breath of courage and learned how to move forward in the face of our fears. In this chapter, we will begin to flow and grow with God's inspired Word on **perseverance**.

Webster defines perseverance as "the continued effort to do or achieve something despite difficulties, failure, or opposition." It is the spirit of perseverance that allows you to persist and keep pressing on no matter the challenges you face. Whenever you make up your mind to accomplish a goal—whether small or great—the enemy will undoubtedly be there to oppose and discourage you. He will try to convince you that you are not strong enough, smart enough, wise enough, or resourceful enough.

Satan will lay down many roadblocks to try and trip you up. He knows that you do not like to suffer, so he will try to make your efforts as painful as possible. You have to learn how to dig deep and find the inner strength to push past the pain to get to your gain.

When you possess a persevering spirit, roadblocks won't deter you. They may slow you down; it may take longer to accomplish your goal and finish what you started; your dream may be delayed, but it won't be denied. Those who refuse to give up and, instead, persist in their efforts find a great reward waiting for them at the finish line. Their success is found not in finishing fast, but enduring to the end.

STAYING THE COURSE

> *I have fought the good fight, I have finished the race, I have kept the faith.*
> (2 Timothy 4:7)

The Christian life is often represented as a race to be won. But before you can *win* the race, you must *begin* it. The Christian race starts when one accepts Jesus Christ as her Lord and Savior. You must believe in Him and repent of your sins. Then, once your race starts, you will need perseverance to stay the course God has for you.

In the verse above, the Apostle Paul was declaring that he had run the race of life set before him and he remained steadfast and faithful in doing so. God has a unique course for each one of us to run. Don't try to run somebody else's race—follow God's good and divine plan for *your* life. You don't get to choose your course in life. If it were an option, I definitely would not have chosen the rugged roads of layoffs and losses I've experienced.

My sister, Daphne, certainly would not have chosen to get breast cancer, but that is a hill that she had to climb on her course. Given a choice, my family surely would not have chosen to lose my dear sister, Andrea. Unfortunately, that steep valley was put on our course.

I am sure that you can think of some hills and valleys that you would like to remove from your course right now. If we could pick our own course to run in life, we would undoubtedly choose the easiest path—one clear of all obstacles. But God knows that trials and tribulations are necessary for the development of our character and spiritual growth.

Your character is tried and tested when times are tough and you are tempted to give up—weaknesses are not revealed while walking down Easy Street. You simply do not know what you are *really* made of until the right set of circumstances tests your character. God uses those trying situations to expose your weaknesses and make you stronger for greater challenges up ahead. Paul teaches us that we can find joy even in the midst of our trials because of the perseverance they produce.

PERSEVERE THROUGH THE PAIN

Not only so, but we also rejoice in our sufferings, because we know that suffering produces perseverance.
(Romans 5:3)

Perseverance allows you to endure your problems and keep pressing forward in spite of them. Life will definitely present you with many difficulties that will test your faith in God. Make no mistake: the enemy will try you and, yes, God will sometimes allow it. The enemy's intentions are bad, but God uses them for your good. You only have to look to Job in the Bible to see how far the enemy will go to try and push you over the edge.

Some Christians have the misperception that the Christian life is supposed to be easy and free from afflictions, but this could not be further from the truth. In fact, the enemy went after Job because he was a righteous man. He wanted to prove that Job was only faithful to God because of the many blessings he received. His argument was "if you take those things away, Job would turn his back on God."

We often don't understand why God allows us to go through certain trials, but our job is simply to trust that God knows best. Know that He will never leave nor forsake you. Job had every problem you could possibly imagine. He lost all his possessions, his children, his friends, his wealth, and health. Job suffered immensely and was in great pain and agony. At one point, his wife suggested that he just curse God and die (see Job 2:9). She was basically telling him to give up on God…and then give up on himself.

That is exactly what will happen, by the way: if you give up on God, you will eventually give up on yourself, because you can't do it without Him. But Job refused to give in to the temptation to turn his back on God. He ignored the bad advice from his wife and held on to his faith. Instead of cursing God and dying, he blessed God and lived! Eventually, God restored Job with a new family and twice as much wealth.

NEVER GIVE UP

What will you do in times of trial? Will you curse God, whine, complain, and blame Him for your situation? Or will you dig deep, entrench yourself in His Word, and hold on to His unchanging hand? Will you refuse to curse God and die, and instead choose to bless the Lord and live? Refuse to give up when the going gets tough.

Job was certainly tempted to give up, and we would have understood it if he did. But his spirit of perseverance and willingness to be patient and wait on God paid off in the end. You may be going through some great difficulties right now. Maybe you feel like nothing is going your way and the world is against you. In your moments of despair and wanting to give up, hold on to the promise that God is with you always. Determine in your spirit that, with the grace of God, you will press forward in the face of your obstacles.

The greatest example we have of perseverance is Jesus Himself. Imagine where you and I would be today if Jesus had decided to quit His mission before it was completed. At any point, Jesus could have decided to come down from that cross. He had the power to save Himself, yet He endured immense suffering and pain because it was part of God's master plan to save you and me.

Before Jesus drew His last breath, He declared, "It is finished." (See John 19:30). Meditate on those three words for a minute. How often are you able to say, "It is finished"? Too often, the three words we say are, "I give up." We think to ourselves, *I can't do this anymore. This is too hard. This is too much work.* We are

INSPIRATION 18: INHALE PERSEVERANCE

quick to throw up our hands in defeat and settle for far less than what is possible, if only we would hold on a little longer.

Be honest. How often are you able to say that you finished what you started? So many times we start projects but fail to see them through to completion. We excitedly set new goals, take one step towards them, and then give up the moment we have to sacrifice or suffer in the least.

Take a moment to think about a project or goal that you started but have yet to complete. Pray and ask God to give you the spiritual will to get back on track. It is never too late to get back on course and finish your race. When you are tempted to give up, draw in a deep breath of perseverance, and keep on pressing on.

Notice that Jesus did not declare His mission complete until right before He died. As long as you are still living and breathing, your race is not over. You still have a course to run, a purpose to fulfill, and assignments to complete. Don't sit around complacent and idle, watching other runners pass you by, as if you have nothing to do. Get up and keep running your race until you reach the end.

PICK UP THE BALL AND RUN WITH IT

My son plays youth football, so I have had the opportunity to appreciate the game and the character it builds in the players. To be successful in football, players must learn how to persevere. The offensive team's goal is to cross into the end zone. The opposing team—the defense—has the goal of keeping the offense from achieving *its* goal. The defense aims to block, counter, oppose, and interrupt the plans of the offense. The moment the ball is in motion, the defense follows that ball intensely and does all it can to take down the player who has it.

As Christians, we have signed up to play on God's team, but we must never forget that Satan has his own team suited up and ready to oppose us every step of the way. His mission is to frustrate our efforts to the point where we just want to get out of the game. As long as you are sitting on the sidelines of life and not actively pursuing your goals, the enemy is not very interested in you—but the moment you decide to go for your dreams (to pick up the ball and run with it), the enemy sends in his team to tackle you.

In football, size can be a great factor used for intimidation. There are some youth boys who are so big they look like they should be playing in the pros, not on a little league team. The enemy knows how to send out his big players to stir up fear in you. If you are wavering in your faith and lacking in courage, you will easily want to drop the ball and run for the sidelines.

Football is not for the faint of heart and neither is the Christian life. When hundreds of pounds of fear are staring you down, that is the time when you must dig deep and find your spirit of courage. Don't drop the ball and run—instead, get a firm grip on it and go for the touchdown.

It is good to know that you are not in this game alone and you are on the winning team. God will protect you and keep you. He will block for you and clear the pathway all the way to the goal line. Even if you get knocked down, God will pick you back up, dust you off, and send you right back into the game. You may get a little bruised in the process, but God will see

INSPIRATION 18: INHALE PERSEVERANCE

to it that you come out with the victory. If you keep pushing, pressing, crawling, and inching your way towards the goal line, you'll eventually experience the sweet taste of victory.

KEEP ON KEEPING ON

We can learn a thing or two about perseverance from our children. When it comes to getting what they want, kids have a determined spirit that will not quit. Advertisers know this full well and use it to their advantage. The parents have the money, but the kids have the power to beg, plead, kick, yell, sulk, and cry until the parents give up the money to buy them what they want. I am normally not so easily persuaded by my son's pleas for things, but I, too, give in to his very consistent and persistent requests at times.

We need to approach the things we want in life with this same level of childlike persistence. In 1 Thessalonians 5:17, we are encouraged to pray without ceasing. This simply means that we are to keep on making our petitions known to God until we get an answer. Do not give up the first time you pray and don't hear from God. Keep praying, keep asking, keep making your requests known before God. We are to constantly approach the throne of grace, asking for God's mercy in everything we do. Even when it seems like God is silent, know that He is there and you always have His ear. Don't give up in frustration when you don't get the answer you want right away.

Keep on asking, and you will receive what you ask for. Keep on seeking, and you will find. Keep on knocking, and the door will be opened to you.
(MATHEW 7:7 NLT)

Could it be that you aren't receiving what you need because you've grown weary and have stopped asking in faith? Maybe you aren't finding what you are looking for because you've stopped searching. Perhaps certain doors of opportunity have not been opened to you because you have stopped knocking.

There have been times when I asked my son to go to another room to get something for me. He quickly returned and told me that the item was not there, that he could not find it. I went into the room, took my time to look and found what I was seeking. My son did not really search for the item. He had simply scanned the room quickly and—when it was not immediately visible—he gave up and declared that it could not be found.

If you wish to find the things you want in life, you will have to develop the patience to seek them out diligently. We should not expect that things will go easy for us simply because we are Christians. If you have been knocking on doors and they still are not being opened, maybe you are knocking too softly. Develop a firm and consistent knock and refuse to give up. If it is in God's will for you, eventually the door will swing open. Be persistent and determined in whatever goals you pursue. You don't have the luxury of giving up easily. Keep on asking, seeking, and knocking—sooner or later your persistent spirit will yield you great returns.

It is time to exhale and release that "I quit," "I give up," "I'm too tired" spirit. Open up and allow God to breathe His spirit of perseverance in you. Inhale and receive the spirit of perseverance that allows you to declare, "I will not quit," "I refuse to give up," "I will go all the way."

INSPIRATION 18: INHALE PERSEVERANCE

Are you willing to go all the way with God? Are you ready to get back in the game of life and pick up your ball and run with it? Do you have the determination to run your race to the end? Remember, the race is not given to the swift; it's given to those who endure to the end.

God will give you what you need to keep on pressing on. The same persevering spirit that would not allow Jesus to quit on you and me is available to you today. Your persevering spirit is closer than you think. Just breathe. Your perseverance is just a breath away.

INSPIRATION 19:
Inhale Purpose

Discovering Your Unique Path and Walking It

> *"For I know the plans I have for you," declares the LORD, "plans to prosper you and not to harm you, plans to give you hope and a future."*
> (JEREMIAH 29:11)

In the previous chapter, we inhaled perseverance. In this chapter, we will begin to flow and grow with God's inspired Word on **purpose**.

Do you know the plans God has for you? They are good plans: to prosper you and give you a great future. You may be at a season in your life where you feel that all of your plans have failed. Nothing seems to be going right and everything you touch seems to fall apart. God promises that He has great plans for you. You may not understand all that you have gone through and what you are currently experiencing may not make sense. But God promises that, in the end, it will all work together for your good. Your hurt, pain, failures, and suffering may seem senseless, but they all serve a purpose in the higher purpose God has for your life. God will use all that you have been through to mold, make, and shape you into the woman

INSPIRATION 19: INHALE PURPOSE

you were created to be so you can go on to do the task He appointed you to do.

God has a reason for everything He creates and continues to breathe life into. He created the entire universe and set everything in its proper position before He created you—but when He created it, He had you on His mind.

Scientists are beginning to understand more and more how this planet is intricately designed in a way to support human life. God created it all in this way not only for you to simply survive, but to thrive. When He made you, He left no detail untouched. He precisely formed, shaped, and designed you into exactly who He needed you to be to fulfill the specific purpose He has for your life. Nothing about you has been left to chance or is a mistake.

God knew every day of your life before you even took your first breath. And as long as you are still living and breathing, God has purpose for your life. If your life no longer served a purpose on this earth, God would no longer be breathing the breath of life into you. It is imperative that you understand this divine truth and inhale God's purpose for you deep down in your spirit.

YOU'RE STILL HERE FOR A REASON

I have an affirmation that I repeat to myself often: "As long as I'm still breathing, I've still got purpose. And as long as I've still got purpose, I will pursue my purpose with a passion." Do you know your purpose and mission in life? Are you pursuing your purpose with a passion? God still has you here for a reason.

You may have experienced a lot of loss in your life. You may have lost your job, your car, your home, your marriage or your financial security. But one thing that no one can ever take away from you is your divine God-given purpose. Without a sense of purpose, you'll wander through life aimlessly and merely exist. Nothing will seem to make sense. But when you understand why you are here and how your life contributes to the greater purposes of God, your life will take on a whole new meaning. Your perspective will change and you'll shift from trying to merely make a living and begin making a life. Once you wake up to your purpose, you can begin to live life fully alive, making the most of every breath you take.

Things may not have always gone according to your plans, but that is okay, because God's plans are better. He knows best. God is not interested in worldly success. He wants you to live a life that has eternal significance. It is possible to be highly successful yet totally unfulfilled. Maybe you are experiencing great success in your life but have a deep feeling that something is missing—a void, an emptiness, a deep yearning for more. You know that you are not fulfilling your purpose and something else is calling you.

Nothing will fill the void in you except the passionate pursuit of your God-given purpose. It is time to put aside your agenda and personal goals and get to understand God's will for your life. You were made for a specific and very special purpose. Your job is to uncover that reason, discover your divine assignment and begin to live life on purpose for God—and there is nothing more potent and powerful than a life lived on purpose.

INSPIRATION 19: INHALE PURPOSE

Jesus gives us an example of a life well lived on purpose for God. He revealed His mission when He said, "I have come that they may have life, and have it to the full." (See John 10:10). Jesus understood His mission on earth and never strayed from it. He was not distracted by critics, enemies, naysayers, or hypocrites. Immense pain and suffering could not deter Him from carrying out His calling.

We know Jesus was in agony when He said, "Father, if you are willing, take this cup from me; yet not my will, but yours be done." Jesus would rather not have endured that experience, yet He stayed on the cross in obedience and submission to his Father's will. He understood that the purpose He was fulfilling far outweighed the temporary pain He was enduring.

Pursuing your purpose may sometimes cause you to suffer and endure things you would rather not experience. God may ask you to go places you would rather not go, do things you would prefer not to do, and say things you would rather not say. Are you willing to step out of your comfort zone to follow your Heavenly Father's will? Will you follow Christ's example and say, "not my will, but Yours be done"?

YOU CAN RUN, BUT YOU CAN'T HIDE

Let's take a look at the book of Jonah in the Bible. One day, the Lord spoke to Jonah, a prophet from Galilee, and instructed him to go to Nineveh to preach to the Ninevites. Jonah was supposed to warn the Ninevites that they must repent of their sins or suffer the consequences.

The Ninevites were one of Israel's greatest enemies, and Jonah was not interested in trying to get them to repent. Instead of following God's command, Jonah ran away from God and took off in the opposite direction. He hopped on a boat headed for Tarshish, hoping to hide out from God. He soon found out that there is no place to hide from God.

At night, God caused a huge storm to come upon the boat and toss the passengers to and fro wildly. The sailors and captain were very afraid and eventually followed Jonah's request to throw him overboard. The sea then immediately returned to calm.

God could have allowed Jonah to die, but instead He sent a great fish to swallow Jonah. Jonah stayed in the belly of that whale for three whole days and nights praying fervently to God and thanking Him for his salvation. God had mercy on Jonah and had the whale spit him onto shore. Then God told Jonah once again to go to Nineveh to preach the message of repentance. This time Jonah obeyed!

There is so much to learn from this great Bible story. The overall message is that you can run, but you can't hide. When God calls, He expects you to answer. You may try to ignore His call, but He has creative ways of getting your attention. A calling from God is not reserved for preachers, prophets, and ministers. He has a calling for each one of his children and you are no exception—He has a special assignment with your name on it.

When He calls you, are you going to run away like Jonah? If you do, don't be surprised if you are suddenly overtaken by a storm and end up trapped in the belly of a whale. God will put you in a position where He has your undivided attention and no place to hide. He could have easily allowed Jonah to be

INSPIRATION 19: INHALE PURPOSE

swallowed up by the raging sea for not obeying his command but, instead, God's grace gave Jonah a second chance. Has God ever given you a second chance, third chance, or even a one-hundredth chance to do what He has called you to do?

Jonah eventually realized that it was easier to follow God's will than to stubbornly do what he wanted. We each have to come to that conclusion for ourselves. After wearing yourself out for so long trying to run from God, you'll learn that it's much better to work *with* Him than *against* Him.

Are you running from your purpose right now? Are you ignoring the calling that God has on your life because you think it's inconvenient and uncomfortable for you? Maybe it's not as glamorous as you want it to be or you can't see how you will make a living doing what God has called you to do. It's time to stop running from your purpose and instead start running *with* your purpose.

IT'S NOT ABOUT YOU

Before we leave this story, let's examine why Jonah ran from God in the first place. Jonah revealed that his motive for running was that he knew God may have mercy on the Ninevites and spare their lives (and he didn't want that for Israel's enemy). After Jonah preached the message of repentance to the Ninevites, they turned from their wicked ways, and God did, indeed, show mercy upon them. Jonah was angry with God for showing compassion to the Ninevites who had, at one time, been very wicked and evil towards the Jews.

Jonah did not want God to use him as part of God's plan to deliver the Ninevites. Before you go judging Jonah, honestly think about it. Are there any people whom you resent and would like to see fail? Would you have a hard time ministering to someone who has hurt or wronged you in some way? Jonah felt this way. He did not want to see the Ninevites receive mercy; He wanted them to suffer. The problem with this way of thinking, though, is that if we all got what we truly deserved, none of us would be saved. We all fall short of God's glory and honor, and it is only by the grace of God that any of us has a pathway to Heaven.

If you have not yet realized it, your purpose is not only about you. It is about who God wants to bless *through you*. God's purpose for you fits into the greater purpose He has for all of mankind. If you are willing, God will use you and put you in a position to be a blessing to others. You do not get to choose your assignment, the position you will be placed in, nor the particular people who will be blessed by your ministry. Your job is to just go where God tells you to go, do what He tells you to do, and say what He tells you to say—God will handle the rest.

Remember, God says He knows the plans He has for you. They are His plans, not yours. You don't get to create the plans; you just carry them out. A soldier in the army does not choose his destination for duty or write his own orders; he simply goes where his orders say to go. He follows the direction of his commanding officer, whether he likes it or not.

God is your Commander-in-Chief and you are on the battlefield for the Lord. Go to God for your marching orders, then take your position on the battlefield and do what you were sent out to do.

INSPIRATION 19: INHALE PURPOSE

APPOINTED AND ANOINTED

You may feel that you are ill-equipped and unprepared to do what God has called you to do. Moses felt this way when the Lord commanded Him from a burning bush to go tell Pharaoh to let God's people go (see Exodus 3:1-10). God had a great plan to rescue the Israelites from the Egyptians. God chose Moses to play a major part in executing that plan and leading the children of Israel into a land flowing with milk and honey. What was Moses' response to this amazing honor by God? He questioned God and asked, "Who am I that I should go to Pharaoh and bring the Israelites out of Egypt?"

God assured Moses that He would be with Moses every step of the way. Moses continued to protest and offered up every excuse he could imagine. One of his excuses was that he was not an eloquent speaker. God responded by reminding Moses that it is God who gave him his mouth. God would speak for him. God answered every protest and even performed miracles to convince Moses that He would be with him. However, Moses still asked God to send someone else. Eventually, God became frustrated and angry with Moses. Moses finally agreed to go when God said Aaron, Moses' brother, could go with Moses and speak for him.

Has God asked you to do something that you feel ill-equipped to handle? Always remember that God anoints those whom He appoints. God will empower and equip you to do whatever it is He has called you to do.

I have questioned God many times on why He chose me to write this book. I was content with just working in the children's story ministry in my church. It is through writing and delivering children stories that the idea for writing a book came about, but the idea did not originate from me. God allowed different people to cross my paths and deliver the message that I should write a book. I thought they were all crazy, and I had no plans on writing a book, but God's plans are not my plans. I eventually had to put aside my agenda and get in line with God's will.

Yes, I initially tried to run like Jonah and hide from His calling, but I quickly learned that though I could run, I could not hide. But that did not stop me from running. I have spent many years and countless nights tossing and turning with the weight of God's will weighing heavily on my heart. I finally realized that God was not going to allow me to rest until I did what He was telling me to do.

I felt like I imagine Moses did when God called him. I continually made excuses why this task was too hard and I just couldn't do it. I questioned who was I to write a book about becoming more when I was still far less than who I needed to be. God reminded me that He calls the least likely people to do some of the greatest works (see 1 Corinthians 1:27). God uses the broken, fragile, and weak to perform some of His greatest works. The reason is simple. When His purpose is accomplished through such weak vessels, it will be obvious that God's mighty hand is at work. God alone will get the glory and draw men unto Him. Stop asking *why* and start asking *what*: God, what do you want me to do with my life?

THE WORLD NEEDS WHAT GOD PUT IN YOU

You were born with talents and abilities that enable you to do certain things very well. God also bestows particular spiritual

INSPIRATION 19: INHALE PURPOSE

gifts upon believers as He pleases. Don't covet or envy anyone else's gifts—be grateful for your own gifts and use the talents that have been given to you.

Your gifts, talents, personality, and experiences all work together to uniquely shape you for serving the role God has assigned to you. Take the time to tally up your talents and see how they play a role in how you will fulfill your purpose. If God gave you a talent, He intends for it to be used to His glory.

But the gifts God gives you are not for you alone—if you are the only one benefiting from your gifts, something is wrong. God blesses you so you can be a blessing to *others*.

In 1 Corinthians 12:12, the apostle Paul begins to draw an analogy between the human body and the body of Christ. Your body is made up of many parts but is united as one. Each part has a particular position and role to play; if one part stops functioning, the entire body will suffer. No one part is more important than another. The parts that seem insignificant usually play a major role in the overall functioning of the body.

God alone has placed each part where it belongs and assigned it a particular function. We are to honor and value the usefulness of each part, no matter how large or small. In this same way, God has assigned you and me particular positions and roles to play in the Body of Christ. Our roles are different, but equally important. Never underestimate your value and importance to the Body. Know that your gifts, talents, experiences, personality, and all that makes you uniquely you are critically needed by those whom you will serve.

It is time to exhale and release any negative thoughts that try to convince you that your life does not matter. Let go of thoughts that you are a big mistake and the world does not need what you have to offer. Inhale and receive into your spirit the fact that God created you *on* purpose, *for* a purpose, and *with* a purpose. You are not insignificant; your life has meaning and the world needs you.

Open up and allow God to breathe the breath of purpose into your spirit. Yield to God and allow Him to fill you with His divine purpose and set you on a path to living life fully alive for Him. Your life filled with divine purpose is closer than you think. Just breathe. Your purpose-filled life is just a breath away.

INSPIRATION 20:
Inhale Passion

Living Life on Fire for God

> *Never be lacking in zeal, but keep your spiritual fervor, serving the Lord.*
> (ROMANS 12:11)

In the previous chapter, we inhaled God's divine purpose into our spirits. In this chapter, we will begin to flow and grow with God's inspired Word on **passion**.

God will inspire you with the passion to pursue your purpose. He will place certain desires, hopes, and dreams in your heart and lead you to care about particular causes and activities. Pay attention to the things you care about most; they will offer clues as to where you should be serving and what God wants you to do.

God wants you to serve Him out of passion and love, not duty and resentment, so whatever you do for God, do it with all your heart. God gives you passion for your purpose so you will enjoy doing what He has called you to do. When you love what you do, you do it with excitement, enthusiasm and exuberance; you are motivated by the pure joy of it, not money, rewards, or recognition. Your passion will fuel and energize you in a way that nothing else can. You do it because you want to, not because you have to.

Passion causes you to put all your heart and soul into something and see it through to completion. This is the type of heartfelt emotion God wants you to have towards the task he has assigned to you. God wants to breathe a fresh breath of passion into your spirit and energize you to pursue your purpose with all your heart.

PURSUE YOUR PURPOSE WITH A PASSION

In the last chapter, I shared with you an affirmation that I repeat to myself often: "As long as I'm still breathing, I've still got purpose. And as long as I've still got purpose, I will pursue my purpose with a passion." Once you fully *understand* God's purpose for your life, it's time to set out to *pursue* it with a passion.

If you lack passion, you won't have the energy and drive necessary to go the distance—the moment anything distracts you or stands in your way, you'll give up and abandon the task. Without passion, you won't have the fuel needed to continuously move forward in the face of obstacles.

Jesus showed us what it means to be truly passionate about a purpose or cause that is dear to our heart. He was passionate about helping and healing people and made that the ministry of His life. He set out on a mission to make people whole again and restore them back into a right relationship with His Father. His deep compassion for people and the heart to serve them gave him the energy to minister to crowds both day and night. He never lost his fire for His ministry and mission in life; it fueled Him all the way to the finish line where He was able to say, "It is finished" (see John 19:30). Do you have the energy you need to run your race and finish your course? Are you passionate enough about your purpose to do whatever it takes to fulfill it?

My dear sisters, how would you describe your life right now? Have trying circumstances, difficult times and one too many disappointments caused you to lose your zest, zeal, and fire for life? Has your life become mundane, monotonous, and routine? Are you living life fully alive or are you just merely existing, going through the day-to-day motions? Have you given up on your dreams and lost sight of the vision God once revealed to you?

Are you just doing what you can to get by and make a living? God wants you to do much more than just make a living. He wants you to put all your energy into making a life that will last forever—to passionately pursue your purpose, and focus on the things that will have eternal consequences. He wants you to embrace each day with eagerness, enthusiasm, and excitement.

WHAT MOTIVATES AND MOVES YOU?

If you are not sure where your passion lies, look back over your life for clues. Examine your past experiences in your career, family life, church service, volunteer work, hobbies, and extracurricular activities. What are you passionate about? What excites you and gets you all fired up? What could you spend hours doing and not tire of doing it? If money were not a concern, what would you do with your life? What do you do that does not feel like work—the thing that causes you to lose all track of time because you enjoy it so much? What sparks

INSPIRATION 20: INHALE PASSION

your interest in a way that nothing else does and gets your heart beating fast when you think about it?

Your childhood can also offer up clues to help you discover your passions and natural interests. Children are uninhibited and free—coloring outside the lines, dressing up, playing make-believe, dreaming big, and believing anything is possible.

What were your dreams back then? Where did your imagination take you? Who did you pretend to be? What did you love to do or hoped you could do some day? Take the time to find out what excites and interests you in order to discover what motivates and moves you like nothing else.

There are two types of motivation: extrinsic and intrinsic. External factors and pressures drive extrinsic motivation—you do it only for reasons outside of you. Examples of extrinsic motivation are: working only for the reward of a paycheck or serving in the church only for recognition.

On the other hand, intrinsic motivation comes from within. This is the type of motivation you should desire, because you will do what you do for the sheer joy of doing it. No one will have to reward you, recognize your efforts, or even acknowledge what you do. You will do it because you love to do it; getting paid or receiving another type of recognition or reward is simply a bonus.

If you have to pay your kids or bribe them with gifts to get good grades in school, they are operating on extrinsic motivation. You may do this for now, but eventually you want to get them to the point where they are internally motivated to strive for excellence simply because they want to be the best they can be. They need to develop an internal drive that will carry them throughout their life.

This is the type of drive that God wants us to have towards the pursuit of our purpose. He wants us to do what we do for Him because we love doing it and we get pleasure out of it. We should take pleasure in serving God and others with our God-given gifts and talents.

TAKE STOCK OF YOUR GIFTS AND TALENTS

Do you have a good understanding of your gifts and talents, or do you believe that you don't have any? God has given us each a set of gifts and talents to be used in our ministry and mission in life (1 Peter 4:10). There are some things that you are naturally good at doing better than other things. We often minimize and downplay our talents to others. We fail to recognize the value of our gifts and don't treasure them as we should.

If you don't know what your talents are, just ask those around you. Because it comes naturally to you, you may not give yourself the credit you deserve, but people around you who see your gift in action will be able to point it out to you.

It took me a long time before I recognized that I was gifted at writing and telling stories to children. I started working in the children's story ministry at my church about twenty years ago. At the time, we were a new church, in service for less than a year. During the worship service, time is set aside to tell the children a story about God. The children come out from the congregation to sit down on the steps in front of the church where someone tells them a story.

INSPIRATION 20: INHALE PASSION

My mother was one of the charter members of the church and already played multiple roles, including doing the children's stories, but she asked me to take over. I was very reluctant at first because I knew nothing about telling stories to children, and I was extremely shy and afraid to speak in front of audiences. I finally agreed to do it and my first story was a hit with the children and adults alike.

We are coming up on our 20-year anniversary, and we can celebrate that our story ministry is still thriving and touching the lives of the children in our church. I feel quite old, because kids who listened to my first stories are now grown and have gone off to college. I was a college student myself when I started in the ministry and worked at it alone for many years, but I am now happy to say that the children's story ministry has grown into a team of storytellers who are all passionate about planting seeds of faith into our children.

Although the stories are supposed to be for the children, over the years, many adults have expressed to me that my stories have moved and inspired *them* and some have encouraged me to write a book to share the stories with the world. It took a while for me to grasp it, but after hearing the same idea from so many people, I finally got it: writing, speaking, and inspiring both children and adults is a gift, and God wants me to use it for his glory.

I am extremely passionate about writing. I write for hours on end and lose myself in it. I have boxes of journals filled up with my writings from over the years. I have not shared most of my writings with anyone—I have been my only audience. I do not write for reward or recognition, but do it simply because I love to do it.

Can I tell you a secret? As a writer, ideas can pop in your head at any time. Over the years, as I would drive places, I would often get inspired with children's story ideas and other inspirations for this book. I could not write because I was driving, so I would call my voicemail and leave a message. I turned on the speakerphone and spoke away. When I made it to my destination, I would check my voicemail, passionately type up the messages, and email them to myself.

I recently checked my old emails. I have *hundreds* of these emails dating back to 2002! Thankfully, I now have a phone with a voice recorder on it to capture all of those ideas. All of those years that I was writing and speaking those messages, no one was looking, no one was listening, and no one was offering me a reward to do it. I did it simply because I loved to do it. It was, and still is, my passion, my gift. What is yours?

It is time to exhale and release any lackadaisical thoughts you have towards life. Let go of any thoughts that convince you that it is okay to merely exist. God created you to live life fully and passionately. Your Heavenly Father wants you to inhale a fresh new breath of passion and start living life on fire for Him. Open up and allow God to fill you with His spirit of passion.

Make a commitment today to begin pursuing your purpose with a passion. Your life filled with divine purpose and passion is closer than you think. Just breathe. Your purposeful, passionate life is just a breath away.

INSPIRATION 21:
Inhale Greatness

Becoming More Than You Ever Imagined You Could Be

Great is the LORD! He is most worthy of praise!
No one can measure his greatness.
(Psalm 145:3 NLT)

In the previous chapter, we inhaled passion. In this final chapter, we will begin to flow and grow with God's inspired Word on **greatness**.

The Lord is the Most High God. He is the Lord of Lords, the King of Kings, and above every name in heaven and on earth. The Lord is great and He is worthy to be praised. His greatness is too vast, wide, and deep to be measured by our small minds. He is the Creator of all creation and we look on in wonder of His workmanship. We can only marvel in His majesty and worship His wonderful name.

There are several names we use to refer to God, but I believe one of the greatest names is the Great I AM. When God commissioned Moses to go to Egypt to free the children of Israel, Moses had a question: "Who should I say sent me?" God replied to Moses, "I Am Who I AM. Say this to the people of Israel: I Am has sent me to you" (Exodus 3:14 NLT).

INSPIRATION 21: INHALE GREATNESS

Later in the Bible, we see that Jesus used the same words to describe Himself to the Jews. The Gospel of John notes seven occasions where Jesus referred to Himself as the great "I Am": I am the bread of life (John 6:35). I am the gate for the sheep (see John 10:7). I am the good shepherd (John 10:11). I am the resurrection and the life (John 11:25). I am the way, the truth, and the life (John 14:6). I am the true vine (John 15:1). I am the light of the world (John 8:12).

The Jews were furious with Jesus for making these claims and wanted to stone Him for blasphemy. At one point, Jesus was talking to them about Abraham and they questioned how could He possibly know Abraham when Jesus was not yet fifty years old. Jesus answered, "I tell you the truth, before Abraham was even born, I AM!" (John 8:58 NLT)

THE SEEDS OF GREATNESS ARE IN YOU

The Jews at that time could not wrap their minds around what Jesus was revealing to them. Jesus was telling them that He existed long before Abraham—and all of mankind for that matter. Jesus is the Son of God and has the very essence and nature of God. He existed with God before the creation of the world, and He is who He is with or without His creation because all things were made by and through Him.

Jesus is the Alpha and the Omega—the beginning and the end—and everything in between. His name is above all names and at the name of Jesus every knee shall bow and every tongue confess that Jesus Christ is Lord. (Philippians 2:9-11)

When you accept Jesus Christ as your Lord and Savior, God sends the Holy Spirit to dwell in you. You then have the spirit of the Great I AM living in you to empower you to live out your life for Him. When you are born again, all old things pass away and you become a new creature in Christ (see 2 Corinthians 5:17). You exhale and release all things that are not of God so you can inhale and receive all things that are of the spirit of God.

God gives you a new heart for serving Him and plants His seeds of greatness in you. You have the seeds to become all that He created you to be and to do all that He destined you to do. He planted the seeds of love, joy, hope, and peace into your heart—you have the seeds of strength, courage, confidence, faith, and perseverance within you. The seeds of grace, gratitude, humility, and freedom have all been placed deep down inside of you by God Himself. You were created for greatness and you were made for more!

A seed represents the potential of what something can become. It is packed with possibility and predestined to grow into its greatness. Within every seed is life and the possibility to grow and become all it was destined to be. An acorn—the seed of the oak tree—is already preprogrammed with everything it needs to become a new oak tree. In order to fulfill its potential, the acorn must be planted in the right soil, given the proper conditions, and allowed time to grow.

You and I are no different. The potential is here and the possibilities are limitless, but we must be placed in the right environment and given the opportunity to grow. Don't beat yourself up because you have yet to become all that you long to be—growing into your greatness and the fullness of who God created you to be will take a lifetime. God wants you to commit your life to becoming a better you. It's a process that takes time, patience, and perseverance.

Will you commit to the process of becoming a better you? Many today are anxious to discover their purpose and do something great for God. The Lord definitely has a great plan for your life, but before you can do something great for God, you need to become someone great *in* God. In other words, God is more concerned with your character and developing you into who He plans for you to be so when the time comes, you will be ready to do what He has planned for you to do. You limit what God can do *through* you when you try to limit what He can do *in* you. So before you ask the question, "God, what do you want me to *do*?" ask the question, "God, who do You want me to *become*?"

BECOMING THE BEST POSSIBLE YOU

Inhaling greatness is not about you being the best in the world at what you do. It's about you becoming the best possible *you*. As you surrender your life to the Great I AM, you will begin to flow and grow into your greatness and discover all that is possible with God on your side. Too many people have settled into a life that is far less than God's best. Do you sense in your spirit that the life you are living is much less than what you are capable of if you were to truly yield to God and allow Him to direct your paths? Are you ready to spread your wings and rise to a new level?

Don't settle for a mundane existence, content to just make a living and survive. God wants you to do so much more than just make a living. He wants you to make a *life* that will last forever. What will be the lasting legacy of your lifetime? What will be your greatest contribution to this world? These questions challenge you to look beyond worldly success to eternal significance. When you shift your focus from success to service, your work will instantly have more meaning.

I love what Dr. Martin Luther King Jr. said, "Everyone has the power for greatness—not for fame, but greatness, because greatness is determined by service." You can be of great service to others by becoming all you were created to be and doing all God anointed you to do. Inhaling greatness is not about fame, fortune, notoriety, and popularity.

You may not be called to execute a grandiose plan that affects people nationwide or worldwide. God may want you to make a great difference in the life of the few students you teach during Sunday School. He may call you to make a great difference in the lives of your own children. If you are a teacher, your destiny may be to make a great change in the way your students think about themselves and their potential to become all they were created to be.

Inhaling greatness sums up what this entire book is about: it's about becoming all you were created to be so you will be in the best position to do all you were created to do. As you become more of who you were meant to be, you'll be in a better position to serve those you were meant to serve.

BEING OF GREAT SERVICE TO OTHERS

Being of great service to others is what true greatness is all about. Back in Chapter 12, when we inhaled humility, we saw how Jesus admonished the disciples as they argued over who would be the greatest among them. Jesus settled the dispute by saying, "whoever wants to become great among you must be your servant" (see Mark 10:43). God is clear about His viewpoint of greatness, and it is far different from how the world measures greatness. While others measure you by your worldly success, God is concerned with your *eternal* significance.

At some point, you will have to stand before God and account for your life and how you used the resources He gave you. He will not be impressed with the number of people you got to work for you. He won't ask about the amount of money you made or the material possessions you stored up. God will have no regard for the positions you held or the rewards you received. He will be interested in these questions: "Did you accept my Son Jesus Christ as your Lord and Savior?" and "Did you use your life to be of great service to others?"

MAKE THE MOST OF WHAT YOU'VE GOT

Jesus told a parable of a man who entrusted his possessions to three of his servants while he left to go on a journey (see Mathew 25:14-30). He distributed the talents of money among them as he saw fit. To one he gave five talents, to another two talents, and to the other he gave one talent. The servants who had five talents and two talents took what was entrusted to them, invested it, and came back with more. The one who received one talent buried it in the ground.

When their master returned, the servants had to account for what they had done with what was entrusted to them. Two of the servants presented what was initially given to them plus the interest they gained. The master told the two men, "well done, thy good and faithful servant. You've been faithful over a few things so I'll make you ruler over many." The servant who buried his money returned back to his master the original amount given to him. His master was furious, took the money from him, and gave it to the servant who had gained the most from his money.

The moral of this story is that when God puts something in your hand, He expects you to do something with it. It is not yours to just hold on to, so don't bury it and hide it away—instead, invest it wisely and turn it into more. God has given you hopes and dreams along with the gifts, time, and talent to accomplish those dreams. What are you doing with what you have been given? Are you investing your time and talents into fulfilling the purpose God has for your life? Are you doing all that you can to hone your skills and develop your craft?

Are you using your time wisely and working towards pursuing your purpose with a passion? Are you watering and nurturing the seeds of greatness God has put in you, or are you neglecting those seeds and sucking the life out of them? Whatever God gives you, He expects you to take it and put it to work.

The servant who was only given one talent of money may have felt that he did not have enough to work with—and you may be feeling the same way right now. You may be thinking, "I don't have enough money, time, talents, power, beauty, or connections to do anything great." But God expects you to work with what you've got. He will take your little and turn it into more, but you have to do your part.

It is unwise to be lazy like that servant and sit on your talents. Use your gifts and talents to serve others and glorify God. Don't bury your dreams and leave them to die. Make a commitment to do all you can with whatever you have.

BURIED TREASURES

It is often said that the most treasured places on earth are the many graveyards around the world. In them lay buried books that were never written, songs that were never sung, inventions that were never created, and countless solutions to problems that were never shared with the world. If you feel that you have buried your dreams and neglected your seeds of greatness, it's time to breathe a fresh new breath of life into them.

Your God, the Great I AM, has the power to resurrect the dead and bring back to life anything that was buried. Just ask Martha and Mary in the Bible. These two sisters had lost their beloved brother, Lazarus. The sisters had been mourning their brother's death for four days when Jesus showed up on the scene.

They were upset with Jesus and told Him that had He come when they first requested, Lazarus would still be alive. Jesus assured them that Lazarus would rise again. He directed them to take Him to the tomb where Lazarus' body laid, then, with only His words, Jesus commanded Lazarus to come out—and Lazarus did rise back to life.

To Martha, Mary, and all of the onlookers, Lazarus was dead and buried and all hope for him was gone. But what they failed to realize is that Jesus is the Resurrection and the Life (see John 11:25). When God chooses to breathe into something, it will awaken and arise to new life. To them, Lazarus was dead, but to God he was just asleep, waiting to be awakened. What dreams have you left buried, waiting to be awakened by the breath of

God? Jesus is the living water. When you drink of Him you will never thirst again. Allow Him to water your seeds of greatness so you can grow into all you were meant to be.

You may be bitter like Martha and Mary because things have not turned out the way you wanted them to. You probably feel that you prayed like Martha and Mary, but God did not show up. Had He shown up when you asked Him to, your dreams would not have died. But if you put your trust in God, you can stop being bitter and start becoming better.

God has the power to breathe new life into anything you thought was dead and buried—but like Martha and Mary, you have to take God to where you laid it. Take God to the place where you buried your dreams. Show Him where you lost all hope and gave up on ever doing anything great for Him.

To your surprise, you'll discover that your dreams aren't dead and buried; they are just planted and asleep, waiting to be awakened with God's breathed Word! They are patiently waiting for God to breathe a fresh new breath of life in their direction in order to call them forth to grow into the fullness of what they were destined to be.

JOSEPH THE DREAMER

Once you uncover your purpose and tap into the passion to pursue it, it's time to create a vision for your life. God says where there is no vision, the people perish (see Proverbs 29:18). He also instructs us to write the vision and make it plain so that he who reads it will run with it (see Habakkuk 2:2).

INSPIRATION 21: INHALE GREATNESS

Do you have a clear and compelling vision for your life? Have you taken the first critical step and written it down? Do you see where God is taking you even if you don't know the exact details of how you are going to get there? Has God given you a big dream and a great vision where you see yourself pursuing your purpose with a passion?

We know of Joseph in the Bible as the dreamer. God gave Joseph a dream that was so big that it seemed unbelievable. He saw his father and brothers bowing down to him in his dream. When he shared his dream with his brothers, they hated him for it. They could not handle his dream because they did not have a dream of their own.

Joseph's own brothers set out to kill him because of his dream. Not everyone will be able to handle your dream, even those closest to you. Joseph ended up in the pit and then sold into slavery after sharing his dream with his brothers.

Be selective with who you choose to share your dreams. It is best to find someone else who is pregnant with promise, then you can encourage the dream in each other. Like Mary and Elizabeth, when you get together with someone else who is pregnant with promise, the baby in you will begin to leap. (see Luke 1:41)

It took many years before Joseph's dream came to pass. First, God allowed Joseph to be put in the pit, sold into slavery, and then thrown into prison. I imagine that Joseph was really confused—God had given him a dream, but what he was experiencing seemed nothing short of a nightmare! Has that ever happened to you? God gave you a big dream, but the life you are living is nowhere close to what God showed you in those dreams.

I can definitely relate to Joseph. As I shared with you previously, God gave me the vision to write this book ten years ago. But soon after dreaming that dream, my life started off in a downward spiral. I lost my sister, my marriage, my job, and my entire retirement savings in less than two years. I was so confused: *This is not the dream you showed me God. This is a nightmare!*

Like Joseph, I had to learn that the enemy does not want the dream to be fulfilled in you. Always remember that while Jesus came to give life, the enemy came to take it away (see John 10:10). While God wants to breathe new life into you, the enemy wants to suck the life out of you.

You may not understand at first why God allows you to be thrown into the pit when He promised you a palace, but if you will stay faithful through it all like Joseph did—growing through the process and becoming better instead of bitter—eventually you, too, will see your dream come to pass. You have to learn how to develop a palace mentality in the midst of your pit situation. You have to go the palace in your mind first, and eventually your behind will follow.

FLOW AND GROW INTO YOUR GREATNESS

I believe that God allowed Joseph to experience all of those trials because they helped to develop Joseph's character and grow him into the person God planned for him to be: to handle the high position he would eventually be promoted to in the palace.

INSPIRATION 21: INHALE GREATNESS

Joseph's dream was far greater than his circumstances and he held on to that big dream and his great God no matter what he was going through. He did not use his unfortunate circumstances as an excuse for not serving others or giving up on his dream. He used his gift of interpreting dreams whether he was in prison or in the palace.

Instead of sulking into a life of bitterness, he grew into a life of greatness. He honed his skills, practiced his craft, and became better and better. In the end, God's dream for Joseph was fulfilled and his brothers did, indeed, bow to him when Joseph was made second-in-command in the land of Egypt.

The thing that strikes me most about this story is how Joseph quickly forgave his brothers for what they did to him and how he was keenly aware that God used it all for His glory. Joseph told his brothers, "You intended to harm me, but God intended it for good to accomplish what is now being done, the saving of many lives" (see Genesis 50:20). Joseph refused to give into bitterness and seek revenge. Instead, he acknowledged that it wasn't about his brothers and what they did to him.

It wasn't even about Joseph and how he was betrayed, lied about and grossly mistreated—it was about something much greater. God was working through him to help save the lives of many. Inhaling greatness is not about you using your talents to stroke your ego and start thinking you are better than others. It is about you humbly submitting your life to the Great I AM and allowing Him to work in and through you to accomplish something great for others.

It is time to exhale and release the mindset that keeps you living at a level far less than God's best. You were made for so much more. It's time to give God your less so he can give you His more. Give God your fears, so He will give you His courage. Give God your insecurities, so He will give you His confidence. Give God your worries, so He will give you His peace.

If you will allow yourself to receive, God will flip the script in your life and turn your less into more. He will give you a life that is more than you ever imagined it could be. Exhale and release all bitterness that keeps you from growing into your greatness and becoming a better you. Inhale and receive the seeds of greatness that your Father, the Great I AM, has planted in you. Allow God to breathe fresh new life into your seeds of greatness and awaken you to the unlimited possibilities that await you.

Take God back to the place where you buried your dreams and ask him to breathe new life into them. Hold on to God's great vision for your life and begin to see yourself pursuing your purpose with a passion and flowing and growing into your greatness. Your life filled with divine greatness is closer than you think. Just breathe. Your life of greatness is just a breath away.

You Were Born To Soar!

> *Do not conform any longer to the pattern of this world, but be transformed by the renewing of your mind. Then you will be able to test and approve what God's will is—his good, pleasing and perfect will.*
> (ROMANS 12:2)

I love the butterfly. It provides the perfect example of transformation and how we are to flow and grow into our greatness in Christ. A butterfly's life cycle consists of four stages, going through many changes called metamorphosis. It starts as an egg that has been born into the butterfly family, but just has not matured yet.

Don't beat yourself up if you have yet to mature to the level you would like. If you have been born again, you are a part of the family and you are destined for greatness. Be patient with yourself. Becoming all God created you to be is a life-long process.

During the larva stage, the caterpillar's main purpose is to eat and grow to the correct size, depending on what type of butterfly it will become. Make sure that you are constantly feeding your mind the Word of God so you can grow your character and become all you need to be to fulfill God's plan for you.

As the caterpillar grows, it becomes too large for its exoskeleton and has to shed its skin. When you enter into the process of becoming more—you grow and become more of who God created you to be and less of who you used to be. You will have to shed some things from your life—those things you have outgrown and no longer fit.

During the fourth and final stage, the adult butterfly emerges. Right before the caterpillar thinks it's about to draw its last breath, it emerges as a beautiful butterfly. Sometimes you may feel that you are gasping for your spiritual breath. Maybe you desperately need a breath of hope, love, joy, or peace. You may be gasping for a breath of courage, confidence, purpose, or passion. A trying situation may have come along and knocked the wind out of you. You may feel that you are suffocating and not able to breathe underneath the layers of masks that you have given in to wearing over the years.

God wants you to know that all hope is not lost. Like the caterpillar, your life is not over; it is just beginning. Through the renewing of your mind, God will mold and make you into who He created you to be. You are to study, pray, and meditate on God's inspired Word day and night and allow it to renew your mind. The only alternative to being transformed by the Word is to be conformed to this world. Mastering the art of spiritual breathing is about learning how to inhale the Word so you can exhale the world.

When it comes time for big change, a caterpillar will form a cocoon. It is in this dark place that the caterpillar experiences radical inward change. You may be in a dark place in your life right now; that is okay. This is the time for massive growth and change. This is the time to exchange your old, less-than-worthy life for God's new, exceedingly abundant life.

This is the time to redefine and reinvent yourself with the help of the Holy Spirit. The transformation process will develop the seeds of greatness in you so you can emerge as the beautiful butterfly you are destined to be. You no longer have to crawl around and live the lowly life of a caterpillar. God has much more in store for you.

If you will submit to the process of becoming more—and stay in the process so you can grow—you will eventually emerge with new wings and soar to new heights with Christ. Like the butterfly, God created you to dwell on a higher level than you may be experiencing right now. It is time to spread your wings and rise up. You are destined to go much higher and farther than the body of a caterpillar can take you; you need the wings of a butterfly.

Thank you for allowing me to guide you on your journey to flowing and growing into your greatness and becoming more than you ever imagined you could be. I pray that you will come out of this process with new, colorful, beautiful wings that take you to places you never thought possible. With God, *all things are possible!*

ABOUT THE AUTHOR

Colette Hope

Colette Hope is founder and director of Colette Hope Communications. She is committed to inspiring and empowering women and kids to flow and grow into their greatness and become all God created them to be.

To accompany this book and assist you in putting these biblical principles into practice in your life, Colette has launched a series of poems and Christian meditations called *A Woman Who Breathes*. Each poem and meditation corresponds to a chapter in this book. Colette has also launched the *Becoming a Woman Who Breathes* workbook series. Each workbook in the series corresponds to a poem and allows you to delve deeper into the meaning of the poem and how to apply it to your daily life. The workbooks contain poetry, scripture, prayers, affirmations, and journaling.

For over 20 years, Colette led the Children's Story Ministry at MCBC in Missouri City, Texas, where she continues to worship. Colette is a proud mother of an energetic and joyous eleven-year-old son, Donnie.

ABOUT THE AUTHOR: COLETTE HOPE

To subscribe to Colette's free inspirational e-newsletter or learn more about her workbooks, poetry, meditations, and other personal development resources and services, visit www.AuthorColetteHope.com.

Let's Stay Connected

SHARE YOUR STORY

Email me at info@authorcolettehope.com and share your story of how you are beginning to exhale and release your *less* in exchange for God's *more*! Let me know how *Inspired To Be More* is helping you to break free and flow and grow into your Greatness.

PARTNER WITH ME

Need a mentor or a coach? I'm ready to help you flow and grow into your greatness. To book your FREE Discovery session today, email me at info@authorcolettehope.com or visit www.authorcolettehope.com.

NEED A SPEAKER?

Are you looking for a dynamic, passionate speaker to captivate your audience? Visit www.authorcolettehope.com to view my media kit and speaking topics. Contact me to discuss your needs.

HAVE A SPECIAL ORDER?

This book, along with the mini-workbooks, poetry, and meditations are available for special quantity discounts when purchased in bulk by corporations, organizations and church groups. For information, e-mail info@authorcolettehope.com or visit us at **www.authorcolettehope.com.**

LET'S STAY CONNECTED

CONNECT WITH ME ON SOCIAL MEDIA:

www.facebook.com/colettehope1

www.twitter.com/colettehope1

www.pinterest.com/colettehope1

www.youtube.com/colettehope1

LET'S STAY CONNECTED

OTHER WORKS BY COLETTE HOPE

Becoming A Woman Who Breathes
Mini-Workbook Series:

Becoming A Woman Who Breathes *With Abundance*

Becoming A Woman Who Breathes *With Love*

Becoming A Woman Who Breathes *With Hope*

Becoming A Woman Who Breathes *With Peace*

Becoming A Woman Who Breathes *With Authenticity*

Becoming A Woman Who Breathes *With Purpose*

Becoming A Woman Who Breathes *With Balance*

Becoming A Woman Who Breathes
Meditation Series:

Becoming A Woman Who Breathes *With Abundance* Meditation

Becoming A Woman Who Breathes *With Love* Meditation

Becoming A Woman Who Breathes *With Hope* Meditation

Becoming A Woman Who Breathes *With Peace* Meditation

Becoming A Woman Who Breathes *With Authenticity* Meditation

Becoming A Woman Who Breathes *With Purpose* Meditation

Becoming A Woman Who Breathes *With Balance* Meditation

A Woman Who Breathes Poetry Readings

Available at *www.authorcolettehope.com*.

www.ingramcontent.com/pod-product-compliance
Lightning Source LLC
LaVergne TN
LVHW051548070426
835507LV00021B/2462